SECRET SPLENDOR

THE JOURNEY WITHIN

SECRET
SPLENDOR

THE JOURNEY WITHIN

CHARLES EARNEST ESSERT

Mystics of the World, Publisher
Longboat Key, Florida

SECRET SPLENDOR
The Journey Within

For information contact:
Mystics of the World
Longboat Key, Florida
www.mysticsoftheworld.com

Book design by Palomar Print Design
Cover photograph by Serena Rockey
Photograph of the author by Michael A. McClure

Essert, Charles Earnest

Secret splendor : the journey within / Charles Earnest Essert.

ISBN 978-1-946362-28-5
1. Mysticism — Miscellanea. I. Title.

TABLE OF CONTENTS

PART ONE

WHAT OR WHERE IS TRUTH?

PART TWO

The Quest for Reality

PART THREE

The Mystic Approach to Life

PART FOUR

Toward Freedom

Publisher's Preface

Charles Earnest Essert was one of the few who experienced and could verbalize the fourth dimensional Reality. His creative masterpiece, *Secret Splendor*, stands alone amid classics in mystical literature.

As a young man, Essert believed that true meaning could only be found through a varied and adventurous outer life and it was to this end that he lived. Caring little for formal education, he traveled with circuses and carnivals, worked in factories and wheat fields, played music, moved restlessly throughout Europe, and took employment where he found it. When World War I began Essert joined the service and found when he reentered civilian life two years later that his focus had changed. He was initially drawn to find success through more traditional channels—seeking money, property and achievement—but during the Great Depression realized that material possessions and outer achievements would never bring security or satisfaction. During these post-war years he was drawn inexorably to ever deeper realms of study—psychology, history, philosophy—reading a book a day, absorbing by force of willpower all the knowledge he felt would bring searched for answers. In the end though, he found these studies only led to a "synthetic product," a mere substitute for Reality.

After a time of despair Essert calls "the abyss" a gradual awakening of intuition and revelation led him to the breathtaking experience he called "a shimmering living radiance," a secret splendor.

Though Essert stated "… there are no words or combination of words which even begin to convey cosmic meanings," he did begin to convey those words and to describe the indescribable. Like few others before or since, he was able to illuminate for readers what it is like to be "fully conscious." More importantly, in *Secret Splendor*, Essert lays out an eloquent framework of study about universal truth for all serious seekers yearning to discover the same universal living radiance.

Always the perfectionist, Essert revised the manuscript many times over the course of his life, thus postponing a definitive completion. It is said he lost his only version of the manuscript. A close friend zealously guarded the only copy of *Secret Splendor* and to her goes due honor for its publication. This is a book to read contemplatively and yet with a child's innate awareness that the world is limitless and wondrous. The universe will never again appear quite the same.

In its commitment to provide mystical literature at the highest level of consciousness, Mystics of the World is pleased to be the publisher of *Secret Splendor*. Though posthumously published, the fullness of Charles Essert's realization pervades each page. We are forever grateful that a mystical masterpiece of this quality is now available.

MYSTICS OF THE WORLD

FOREWORD

PERHAPS THERE IS NO stranger anomaly than this, that having life within ourselves, and having the capacity of self-awareness, we do not know what life is. At least we do not know what it is in its essential or ultimate nature. We do not know what occurs during the phenomena of birth and death, how apparently lifeless elements are wrought into cell structures and endowed with livingness and intelligence, or what becomes of these sentient qualities when the cells disintegrate. In short we do not know what it is that forms our own bodies, what it is that makes us think and act.

We call this essence life but this is merely a tag, a name; the essence-itself is a baffling mystery. We have countless ideas, theories, beliefs about life; we have many explanations of the manner in which it expresses itself; we have an extensive knowledge of biological forms, but apparently we are bound by certain mental limitations which do not permit us to know cause. Giving it a name—life, mind, energy, spirit—does not solve the mystery. Names, ideas, permit us to think about life objectively, to speculate, but if we face the matter squarely we are compelled to admit that our knowledge of life is purely hypothetical.

If we are religiously-minded we may say that life and spirit are synonymous, and that this spirit-life is infinite, omniscient, eternal. If we are scientifically-minded we may say that the universe is powered by an impersonal energy which is governed by mechanical laws. In either case we will find a great deal of evidence to support our belief, but in both instances we start with a hypothetical idea. Around this idea we build a supporting framework of similar ideas and as the structure becomes solidified we lose sight of its hypothetical nature. We accept our mental creations as realities.

As a rule this kind of knowledge satisfies us since we are not greatly concerned with what life is, but with the problems of existence. Strangely enough, we believe that the latter can be solved without an understanding of life-itself, or we assume that life's purpose is revealed by our civilization, by the inventiveness of the mind, the development of the intellectual faculties and the refinement of the moral nature. These conclusions are so obvious, so logical, and so generally accepted that nothing short of a catastrophe can awaken us to a realization of our hypothetical existence.

Life provides these catastrophes. Time and again we are shocked into a realization of the unreality of rational existence. During the crises of life—when we are confronted with loss, the death of a loved one, with inconstancy of affection, with betrayal of friendship or trust, with failure or the realization of our incapacity—we become painfully aware of our illusions. During such moments we are endowed with penetrating perception and we see clearly. Without resorting to analysis we perceive the emptiness of our beliefs, the inadequacy of human knowledge, the futility of struggle. Ambition loses its hold and for a time the world as we have known it seems unreal and undesirable.

These crises are considered abnormal; they are mental illnesses from which we must recover as quickly as possible. So we cast about for new purposes, try to awaken the old ambitions, or plunge desperately into some form of activity hoping to gain respite from the pain of these disillusioning periods. We must allay the fever of discontent, get back into the competitive struggle or lose ourselves in altruistic service. In short we try to regain the normalcy of racial consciousness, hypothetical and illusory as it may be.

Now a crisis has no existence per se; it is an intensification of a more extended or chronic illness. Through the heat of fever, nature seeks to destroy the poisons which have accumulated over a long period of time. If the fever is dampened, nature's benevolent purpose is thwarted and the results may be disastrous.

The mental illness with which we are afflicted is a dualistic rationalism—a form of consciousness which creates and accumulates illusory ideas about life and accepts them as reality. These beliefs, religious or scientific, materialistic or idealistic, moral or amoral, stem from the ancient concept of duality—the primitive concept of man separate from and opposed by an external life-force. It is our hypothetical, dualistic beliefs which nature seeks to destroy in the fever of emotional crises.

Intellectual acceptance of the idea of unity does not alter our racial or subjective realization of duality. Each of us has countless subjective beliefs which are impregnated with the idea of dualism. Science itself is the culmination of our dualistic attitude; it represents our most intelligent efforts to overcome a supposedly external nature. Our religions are based on the same realization of duality; we objectify life or the source of being thus making it external and foreign.

We are no longer primitive. We have developed a relatively high sensitivity, a complex nervous system, the capacity for feeling deeply. But we are still engulfed in the darkness of intellectual dualism. Our knowledge consists of hypothetical ideas, theories and beliefs which permit us to speculate about life and its purposes, which compel us to struggle against life in an effort to make ourselves secure in an alien and unfriendly world, but we cannot get at the heart of the mystery. This is the nature of our illness of which the crises of life are but crucial, disillusioning periods.

We cannot cure our mental illness by running away from the disclosures of our insufficiency, by turning to religious or scientific authorities when life itself is destroying illusion through the flame of a more penetrating awareness. We will never discover life through an objective, scientific approach, through an accumulation of inferential ideas. Nor will we discover it through objective experience, for our experiences are based on the subjective illusion of duality. Our interpretation of the meaning and purpose of experience may be logical but it cannot be true since it is based on the realization of separateness.

There is within us a life-essence which is true. It may be neither good nor evil, moral nor immoral, just nor unjust, progressive nor unprogressive for these are inferential conclusions of a dualistic logic. The fact that experience corroborates these conclusions means little, for experience will always harmonize with our subjective beliefs. Life-itself may be illogical, non-striving; contemplative rather than purposive; spontaneous rather than calculative. Whatever it may be in its essential nature it is true, but we cannot discover this trueness through the creation and accretion of hypothetical ideas which are based on the subjective realization of duality. It can be discovered and known only through a process of disentanglement—through an intensity of awareness which strips the mind of its illusions.

If life has a purpose which can be expressed in words, that purpose must be related to what we call awareness. The purpose, let us say, is the production of an organism which will be conscious of life in its totality, of its trueness. Of necessity, such a form of awareness would be direct, intuitive; it would contact and comprehend life in its fullness and without the distortion of imaginary ideas. Further, unlike our present form of consciousness which is finite and relative, the intimate form of consciousness would be cosmic or universal.

Our moments of most intense awareness, of truly discriminating perception, are the frequent crises of normal existence. During such periods we are rudely awakened from the stupor of ordinary consciousness. We become acutely aware of self, of the illusory nature of our beliefs and the limitations of autonomy. What would happen if we did not run away from the pain of disillusionment—if we pursued a course of relentless questioning during the periods of great dissatisfaction? The periods would be lengthened, of course; the mental conflict and emotional fever would become even more unbearable, but as the intensity of conflict increased so would the intensity of awareness. The very conflict would produce a sharpened discrimination, a heightened sensitivity, an altered psyche. Without rational analysis we would begin to perceive the deceptiveness: of our mental illusion. The whole structure of subjective beliefs would be consumed—these dualistic beliefs which now insulate us from a direct knowledge of life-itself. In the heat of this inner conflagration there would be suffering, but out of it would be born a new kind of awareness, direct, intuitive, cosmic.

The discomfort, the unrest, and the penetrating awareness produced by disillusionment can be quickly assuaged by the creation of new interests, but these objective interests are merely palliatives; they do not cure the illness. Sooner or later we must face another crisis and then another. If nature's intent is to produce a fully conscious being in whom awareness is universal rather than particular we may expect these crises to become more frequent and more intense. Until we become "sick of this sickness," this primitive dualism, and are willing to face life courageously we must suffer the results of our ignorance. We cannot escape conflict by creating or adopting "positive" philosophies about life. We merely prolong our suffering, postponing the inevitable conflict which will liberate us from our hypothetical existence. Until we become intensely dissatisfied with our incompleteness, with traditional knowledge and our futile attempts to control an infinite life-force which we do not understand, we cannot achieve that sensitiveness which makes direct, intuitive apprehension possible.

In the following essays there has been an endeavor to show why we cannot discover cause, life, intelligence through scientific or philosophical methods, but how we can know the seemingly unknowable through increased awareness, or a greatly heightened sensitivity.

The key to understanding is simply a recognition of our arrested psychic development—the realization that intellectual consciousness is not life's supreme achievement. For with this dissatisfaction, which arises from the recognition of the limitations of our present status, comes a heightened awareness which destroys illusion. Out of the pain of disillusionment, the travail of intensified self-consciousness, the desire to stand alone and unsupported by the fiction of the intellect, comes a new consciousness. One is inducted into a world of secret splendor, a form of awareness which may well be life's ultimate objective since it is unitary, causal, infinite.

PART ONE

WHAT OR WHERE IS TRUTH?

1

TRANSCENDING DUALITY

IN THE BROADEST SENSE of the word all men and women are truth-seekers. We are all curious concerning the world in which we live. We want to know what makes it "tick," why nature behaves as it does; we are continually asking "why?" and there seems to be no saturation point in our thirst for knowledge.

Somewhere in the journey of life we are confronted with the question of purpose. We wonder whether our lives are really necessary to the whole, whether the seemingly insignificant parts we play have any cosmic meaning. We wonder whether there is a supreme goal toward which we are moving—some ultimate objective which might make the unending struggle of competitive existence worthwhile.

There are times when the thirst for this kind of knowledge and the feeling of incompleteness are very depressing, when the duties and pleasures of life have little significance. What we have secured, what we have done, what we have become are not sufficient. We may not always be conscious of our lack, yet the sense of incompleteness is never entirely dispelled.

It is here that we become truth-seekers in a stricter sense of the word, for we are brought face to face with the really important questions of being. We want to know who we are, why we are here, whence we came and whither we are bound, in the spiritual rather than a biological or historical sense. Is the human Soul a myth or a reality? Is there actually continued existence after death? Can these and similar questions be resolved—can we know the truth?

Many thinkers, both ancient and modem, hold that such queries are unanswerable. We may speculate regarding the nature of the Soul, its origin and destiny, but we cannot penetrate to the core of the mystery. Others have provided reasonable answers which range from purely materialistic theories to abstract metaphysical hypotheses.

When we examine the various philosophies of the world with a critical mind the very conflict of opinion tends to make us more uncertain. It seems that the more earnestly we seek for the true answers the more we are constrained to believe that truth is beyond human comprehension.

There is one thing, however, upon which most thinkers agree: life is a battle, a conflict of opposing forces. Strife and unrest, it is affirmed, are inherent in life itself and therefore we cannot experience lasting peace or satisfaction. These qualities are the ferments, or the leavening agents of life and without them there could be no progress.

If this is true there is no point in seeking peace, or the realization of completeness and perfection. We are automatically doomed to an existence wherein we continually strive but never arrive. In all probability, then, the great queries of the intellect are unanswerable.

Human experience seems to give the stamp of validity to the above conclusions. Apparently we cannot rise above opinions or beliefs regarding the nature of the Soul, and perfection is nothing more than an ideal— something to be aimed at but never achieved.

On the other hand there is a doctrine which is older than the oldest philosophies, its mystic origin unknown.

The basic tenets of this 'great doctrine' have been proclaimed by the avatars or messiahs who have appeared from time to time. The presentation of the doctrine, or teaching, has naturally varied to fit the needs and understanding of people living in different environments at different periods of time, but basically the teachings of all messiahs have been the same.

All have affirmed that the Soul of man is the great Reality; that it can and will reveal its mysterious secrets; that perfection and wholeness can be realized through conscious union with the Soul; that struggle and ferment are *not* inherent in life itself but are part and parcel of the particular form of consciousness which man has achieved, and which man must somehow overcome if he would experience wholeness and perfection.

According to this doctrine the mysterious force we call life is serene, non-competitive, changeless and perfect. Above all it is unitary and indivisible. There is but one life and it is both harmonious and eternal.

Because of the indivisible unity of this life there cannot be a separate existence. Each seemingly diverse portion is the whole; man and the cosmos are one. Furthermore, man can realize this unity and thus experience wholeness and perfection. But not by an intellectual process; it is the intellect which produces the illusion of separateness or duality.

If we would achieve this cosmic unity and the illumination which answers all questions regarding the nature and destiny of the Soul, we must transcend the intellect. Our present form of consciousness (intellectual or rational consciousness) is entirely dualistic; it does not permit us to realize oneness. All things are known to us in pairs of opposites, i.e., as positive and negative, good and evil, sickness and health, life and death, etc. This conception of opposites is an inescapable condition of rational consciousness. In order to reason we must discriminate, discover likenesses and differences, set up two forces in opposition to each other. This is the manner in which the intellectual mind works, and it cannot function otherwise.

But it does not follow that these opposing forces actually exist. It simply means that this is our method of obtaining a rational understanding of an unknown universe. It may well be that the universe is not rational, and that a higher form of intelligence might be counter-rational or super-rational.

This conclusion we must accept if we hope to understand the doctrine advanced by the great avatars. For according to Jesus and all other great spiritual teachers, the Soul, or the infinite phase of our Being, does not *think* as we do. If we have not given the matter special consideration we probably assume that rational consciousness with its endless conception of opposites is the only form of knowingness, and that a supreme being must think in much the same manner as we do but upon a higher level.

Jesus indicated the fallacy of this belief by saying that "The sun shines on the just and the unjust," implying a love, or a form of consciousness in which there is no distinction between our so-called opposites. Gautama said that in the eternal "There is neither high nor low." Chuang Tze affirmed that "In Tao there is neither beginning nor ending, first nor last." All imply that there is a form of cosmic consciousness in which the conception of opposites is unknown.

This form of consciousness cannot be similar to our own. It cannot be rational, cannot employ ideas, discriminate or make decisions, for all such mental operations demand the use of opposites. Of necessity this higher form of consciousness must be other than a thinking state, wholly unlike and vastly superior to human or intellectual consciousness.

Just how different it must be, may be judged from the often reiterated statement of all avatars that it is possible for us to experience eternal life—to realize existence which is not conditioned by the opposing concepts of birth and death. If this is possible, it is possible only through a different form of consciousness than we have thus far achieved as a race, for birth and death are indeed realities and the main conditioning factors of existence.

Intellectually we may conceive the possibility of eternal life but we cannot *realize* it. We experience life as a limited arc—a curved line between the two points of birth and death. If it is possible to experience a beginningless and endless existence then we certainly do not see the world as it really is; something is wrong with our present form of consciousness. As Saint Paul phrased it we "see through a glass darkly," the glass being reason or the intellect. And as he intimated, there is no point in attempting to clean the glass, i.e., in attempting to *reason* more accurately. We must learn to see without the glass, "face to face" with Reality.

2

LEAVING REASON BEHIND

ONE OF THE GREATEST of all mysteries is hidden in
the premise that we can overcome the last and most terrifying of all enemies, death. It is a mystery which science and
philosophy have been unable to solve, for reasons which I
shall try to make clear.

But first let us differentiate between the idea of immortality and the realization of eternal life. Belief in immortality is quite general but this belief does not free us from
the fear of death. It strips away some of the terrors of the
unknown when we approach it, or when our loved ones die,
but life after death is still a matter of faith, the phenomenon
of death an inexplicable mystery, and continued existence a
matter of speculation. And strong as our belief in immortality may be, we fear death. The suggestions of science and
metaphysics that death is biologically unnecessary raise the
hope that we may find the elixir of life and live forever.

The promise of the great avatars is not that we can
escape the phenomenon of death, for having been born on
the material plane we must likewise die a physical death.
But while we are here we may transcend the limits of
intellectual consciousness with its faulty, dualistic notions
regarding the reality of birth and death and thereby achieve
the realization of our unity with Cosmic Life.

This realization of unity with Cosmic Life comes
with an unexpected and subtle expansion of consciousness

7

whenever certain requirements have been met. By a mystic transition one is inducted into the realm of infinities; the veil of nescience is withdrawn and intellectual limitations fade away as new Soul-faculties are quickened into activity.

By and through the great faculty of intuition, one becomes clairvoyant and clairaudient in the highest spiritual meaning of the words, and the hidden significance and purpose of all created things is revealed directly. That is, one *becomes* the thing contemplated, is unified with it in consciousness, and thus shares its cosmic secrets. Without taking thought one knows all things by the simple process of self-realization. Through the avenue of infinitely powerful Soul-senses a hitherto invisible world is revealed—a world of amazing beauty and unity.

Opposites cease to exist, either as intellectual concepts or experienceable realities. The awareness of diversity in nature gives way to the perception of profound and simple oneness. Thus past and future cease to exist. There is nothing but an eternal *now*. One realizes that there is but one life and that he or she is that life in its totality. There is no longer speculation concerning existence after death nor before birth. One realizes total or infinite existence rather than immortality—an existence which had no beginning as well as no ending. The life of which one is conscious is infinite, unbroken, self-existent; unconditioned by birth or death or any other intellectual ideas. It is the great unopposed Reality.

This transition to a higher form of consciousness which permits us to view the world "without spectacles" as it were, but through Soul-senses which penetrate the outer crust or form of things is the basic theme of the 'great doctrine.'

Its true purpose is to lead mankind from rational or mind-consciousness to a much higher form of existence which might be termed Soul-consciousness. But the real significance of the 'great doctrine' has become obscured; we have lost it in our attempt to make an infinite universe fit into our little rational mold. We no longer realize that the next step in our cosmic journey is toward a field of consciousness which is not rational but infinite. Thus we strive to make religion itself rational or scientific.

For reasons which will become clearer as we proceed, this higher form of consciousness does not and cannot result from intellectual development. Development of the intellectual faculties intensifies mind-consciousness and establishes more definite boundaries of rational, scientific beliefs, beyond which it becomes increasingly difficult for us to pass. To a certain extent this is a matter of common knowledge; we perceive that the more scientific-minded a group of people becomes, the more skeptical that group becomes concerning the existence of a super-rational deity.

True religion, as I shall demonstrate, is a worship of the *unknown;* it is evidenced by an affinity for the mystical. The universe in which we have our being is infinite, but due to certain limitations in our faculties of perception we cannot comprehend the infinitude. However, we begin to sense the infinite whenever we welcome and cultivate a mystical appreciation of the world. I use the word here in its commonest meaning; Webster's definition for mystical is "Having a spiritual meaning, reality or the like, neither apparent to the senses nor obvious to the intelligence."

This mystical attitude is altogether different from the intellectual curiosity of the scientifically-minded, and it is a

far more advanced stage of mentality. The essential difference between the two attitudes is that the scientist seeks a
rational explanation of the unknown and is satisfied when
he can reduce his observations to a formula or hypothesis;
the mystical-minded individual hopes to go beyond rational
explanations, to penetrate to the very heart of the unknown,
realizing that the mystery itself must be super-natural and
super-rational.

Up to a certain point in our development the cultivation
of the rational faculties is absolutely necessary. Reason lifts
us above a still lower level of consciousness which we might
term "emotional-consciousness"; it enables us to become
self-conscious beings, to realize our individuality. However,
there is a point beyond which reason is not an emancipating
agent, and beyond that point, it becomes a tyrant, weaving
a web of enslaving beliefs about the self which may bind it
forever to the wheel of opposites, which is the "great wheel
of birth and death."

Reason is unquestionably the highest faculty of the
mind, but we err when we assume that it is the highest
faculty of our Being. Beyond the intellect is the vast,
unknown region of the Soul with faculties and powers of
unimaginable magnitude. It is the possession of these latent
faculties which enables us to contact and comprehend the
infinite. A "mystic" is one who has attained the use of these
faculties to some extent. He is not necessarily a recluse; he
may take part in the finite affairs of mankind, but he is also
en rapport with the infinite world of the wondrous and is
guided by the superior wisdom of the Soul rather than the
rational conclusions of the intellect.

By means of these super-faculties of the Soul the
mystic is able to comprehend infinity, to understand cosmic

meanings and purposes. By means of the intellect he is able to transform such realizations into finite actions.

By means of the intellect alone man is constrained to rely upon reason, and all progress must be by trial and error. Thus the salvation of mankind is not contingent upon further development of the intellectual faculties but in freedom from them. For no matter how perfectly we learn to reason we remain finite beings, bound to a plane of experience where the method of trial and error is inescapable, and where it is psychologically impossible for us to know— to rise above opposing beliefs.

Having achieved selfhood or mature self-consciousness we have arrived at a point where reason has served its chief purpose, and beyond which it tends to become an enslaving agent, moving us irresistibly toward the frigid and unholy region of intellectualism.

Reason has emancipated us from the lowly realms of instinctive and emotional consciousness by virtue of its greater power. Instinct itself sought to bind us, to hold us within its sphere of influence, to keep us on the level of the lowest forms of life. We did not lift ourselves "by our bootstraps." Slowly and laboriously we struggled upward with the aid of a higher faculty, reason.

We cannot lift ourselves "by our bootstraps" now. Reason can no more transcend the limits of its field of influence than instinct could transcend its field. Instead of aiding us in our upward climb, reason, like instinct, will attempt to keep us locked within its sphere.

The intellect must be subjugated, humbled, rejected as the instrument through which we can know truth. It has its place and purpose in our lives just as the subordinate forces of instinct and emotion have theirs, and it will assume its proper role once we have forced it to abdicate the throne.

If we are to achieve a more advanced state of consciousness we must learn to contact and depend upon a higher faculty than reason—a faculty which does not cognize opposites, which does not deal with ideas, which is incapable of argument and does not attempt to persuade, and which is native in the mystic realm of *cause*. This great faculty is intuition, the amazing and incomprehensible faculty of the Soul which reveals the world of the wondrous. In order to tap this higher faculty we must set out in a new direction, leaving the rational world with its faulty, finite ideas behind us. At least we must do so if we hope to experience wholeness.

3

ONLY TRUTH IS CHANGELESS

MANY OF US HAVE ALREADY set out in this new direction but as Ouspensky points out "The tragedy of our questing is that we know not what we are seeking." We call it truth, yet the longer and more earnestly we pursue it the less able are we to define it, or to put our mental fingers on it and say with final conviction, this is the ultimate.

It is only at the outset of our quest that we are certain about the nature of truth. At first we accept certain new ideas as true, but if we continue the search we eventually discover that the ideas we accepted so whole-heartedly yesterday do not hold good for us today. We justify this condition by saying that our understanding has changed, and we believe that we have moved a little closer to the ultimate reality.

It cannot be denied that our understanding changes from day to day, but let us ask ourselves whether it is our understanding of truth that changes or simply our understanding of ideas. For if truth can be encompassed or expressed by means of ideas it is not such an elusive thing after all. If this be so there is no need of attempting to go beyond the intellect in order to find out who and what we are, whence we came and wither bound; no need in going further in our search for the Soul, for God. Ideas concerning the Soul and God are legion. We need only eliminate those which are obviously false and we will have truth corralled. We can

13

engrave it in stone or bronze, or better still set it up in book form and distribute it among the nations of the world. Thus the salvation of mankind would be assured.

Were this at all possible international unity could be achieved almost overnight; poverty, disease and war would quickly disappear from the face of the earth. Fear would vanish from the hearts and minds of men and the long expected millennium would have arrived.

Strangely enough there are millions of men and women to whom all this does not appear absurd. There are innumerable religious sects that believe they have the "truth, the whole truth, and nothing but the truth." The great trouble, of course, is that their versions of it differ. In other words they have nothing but ideas about truth. They may be thoroughly convinced that their ideas are the right ones, but the very divergence of beliefs which exists among them is evidence of error.

As a matter of experience we know that our ideas about truth are not dependable. We, too, may have convictions which serve as anchors in an uncertain world. But at the same time we know that God and the Soul are inexplicable mysteries in spite of our beliefs.

Further, we know that our realization of truth, insofar as we are able to realize it at all, is not subject to change whereas our understanding of ideas is always changing. Identity, for instance, or the realization of Self-hood may be catalogued as truth. It is a phenomenon which cannot be changed or destroyed by logical argument. Within us there is something which affirms "I AM." Let us call it Reality or Truth since it alone is "changeless in the midst of change." If we trace back through the days of our lives we find that identity has never changed. Our environments change, our minds and bodies change, our understanding and emotional natures change, but the mystic inner self which affirms "I AM" is ever one and the same.

On the other hand our ideas about self, about the world, about our capacities and our relationships with other people change from day to day, or from moment to moment.

Truth, if we discover it, will have this characteristic: It will be analogous to the self in that our realization of it will be the same yesterday, today and tomorrow. Furthermore, each person's realization of it will be the same. Your realization of Self-hood, or of the fundamental reality which expresses itself in the words "I AM" is exactly the same as mine, the same as the postman's or the butcher's.

Our ideas about Self-hood will differ, and both yours and mine will change from day to day, but our realization of the underlying reality is the same. For you it is "I," for me it is "I" every waking moment of our lives.

If we accept the doctrine of a cosmic being whose name, according to the Hebrew scriptures, is "I AM"—an infinite "I AM" which expresses Itself through the instrumentality of human consciousness—we will see why the realization of Self-hood is a realization of truth, and why it must be the same for all rational beings.

This "cupful of truth," our personal realization of the cosmic "I" or Cosmic Being, is the extent of our intellectual realization of truth. This realization cannot be destroyed nor can it be changed, but if we would go beyond this finite realization we must go beyond the intellect.

Let us distinguish between the *realization* of self and our *ideas* about self and we have taken a long step toward the discovery of truth. Ideas are controversial, dualistic, antagonistic; truth is unitary, indivisible. Ideas are ever-changing, growing, diminishing, dying; truth is changeless, eternal. It is human fallacy to believe that the latter can be known or expressed through the medium of the former. The ideas, aspirations, emotions of a lifetime are closely associated with the inner self, but in the very literal meaning of the word they are extraneous to the self. They are tools for self-expression but they tell us nothing of the real mystery concealed in the changeless "I." They tell us nothing regarding its origin, its nature, its substance, or its destiny.

Moreover, we will not be able to solve the mystery by accepting new ideas about it. To say that it is the Soul is simply giving it another name. To say that it is Spirit gets us exactly nowhere since we have merely substituted the word spirit for the pronoun "I." To say that it is eternal means little since we cannot comprehend the extent of eternity. The words with which we describe it—changeless, cosmic, unitary, indivisible, self-existent—are incapable of producing an active realization of the mystery itself.

But these ideas do one thing for us: They help us realize what it is not. At least we begin to realize that truth and our ideas about truth are two entirely different things, and that the intellect is incapable of grasping more than the cupful of reality which we call the realization of Self-hood.

Science and philosophy readily admit that our knowledge of the world is relative, and generally speaking we realize that all ideas are contingent upon other ideas, which in turn are contingent upon other ideas, and so on without end. This means that all human knowledge is relative and dependent upon intellect, acceptable and understanding, not separable.

At the same time we know that truth must be absolute, changeless, the same yesterday and forever. It cannot be modified in any way, cannot be dependent upon something else, not even human understanding. If perceived at all it will of necessity appear the same to all persons who perceive it, untempered by differences in human mentality. In this respect it is different from ideas, for the latter depend upon intellectual acceptance, understanding and interpretation. Truth, like Self-hood, is universal and changeless; it will not be realized differently by different men and women.

Too long have we reasoned that ideas represent truth and that truth can be discovered little by little and known through the medium of ideas. We have reasoned thus because we think the intellect is a knowing instrument. The intellect is a very important part of our being but in the strictest sense of the word it is not the knowing faculty. It enables us to *believe*—to believe in this idea, or that one, (to believe in the idea of immortality or to believe in the idea of extinction upon dissolution of the body) but it does not permit us to know the truth.

The intellect enables us to compare and contrast ideas, to select those which appeal to us as the most reasonable in accord with our experience, to build a strong conviction of "rightness" which we call a "belief," but it cannot go beyond this. We may fortify our beliefs with scientific facts but this does not change their status, for these facts are nothing more than relative ideas which may be negated tomorrow by the discovery of new facts.

4

ENTERING THE FOURTH DIMENSION

OUR MAJOR DIFFICULTY in seeking to understand the mystic nature of truth is that we do not realize clearly enough that we are endeavoring to know an infinite magnitude with a finite instrument. This is an impossibility, like trying to dip up the waters of the oceans in a tea-cup. The single cupful of truth we can realize, but the vast expanse and depths with its unending mysteries we cannot know. If we are ever to discover truth in its fullness we must acquire the use of a different instrument. The intellect does not have the capacity for grasping an infinite magnitude.

We have invented words which indicate and to a very limited degree describe an infinite magnitude, but these terms merely point to a possibility which is intellectually inconceivable. The words "eternal life" for instance, indicate a possible condition or phenomenon, but our most abstract thought about the matter cannot carry us beyond a realization of beginning and end, or birth and death. We speak of the infinite possibilities of the human mind but we do not and cannot realize the meaning of our words; we simply imply that the possibilities are beyond our conception.

Naturally there are differences in the conceptual capacities of individual minds, but all are limited to finite realizations. The world as we know it with our present faculties is finite; everything about it is limited and relative. Yet we believe that the universe is infinite. What this "infiniteness"

19

might consist of—whether it is simply an unlimited extension of a finite world or whether the infiniteness might
consist of a dimensionless point which has no extension in
space—we do not know. But if we give the matter any consideration at all we are forced to conclude that an infinite
universe must be unlike anything known to us through the
medium of ideas.

Ideas, let us remember, are finite, relative, subject to
change. To be infinite a magnitude or quality would have
to be changeless and timeless. It could not grow, expand,
evolve, diminish. It could not become something else. To
be infinite a magnitude would have to be all things in their
entirety; nothing could exist outside of nor apart from it,
nothing "new" could be born within it nor could any change
proceed within it. The possibility of change is precluded by
the very nature of infinity; it could not become less, nor
more, nor could it undergo any kind of a transformation
since the "less" and the "more" and all other possibilities are
contained within it.

In other words an infinite magnitude could not change
as the world and all things in the world *appear* to change.
Thus in contrast to an infinite reality such as truth or the
universe our perception of a changing world must be untrue.

This is rather a startling conclusion for it seems to us
that the one thing upon which we can depend is change.
There is a familiar saying which expresses this very human
and rational conviction, "everything is always changing."

It is true that we perceive motion, that we experience it
as growth, and that we can measure it by means of instruments which we have devised for the purpose. But it does
not necessarily follow that we perceive the reality of things.
The world in which we live, like truth, may be changeless

and eternal. In fact if there is such a thing as infinity, the world and truth are identical and synonymous since there can be but one infinite magnitude, call it what we will.

The only way by which we can begin to understand this paradox of a changeless world which presents itself to our minds as an ever-changing phenomenon is to realize that there must be certain limitations in our faculties or organs of perception. If the universe is infinite it is likewise change-less and eternal, therefore we do not see it as it is. To state it differently, if the universe is actually infinite then our perception and our knowledge of it is illusory, and the illusion arises because of limitations in our sensory apparatus.

This does not mean that our sense organs do not function properly within their range of sensitivity. Within their range they are accurate enough, but this range is very limited. For instance, cats and horses are far more sensitive to light than we are, for they are able to see quite well in the dark. Most quadrupeds have greater sensitivity to sound waves than we have and are able to hear not only better, but to hear more; animals respond to sounds of intensely high frequency, sounds which are wholly inaudible to the human ear. Some species like the dog, the otter, and the deer have an unbelievably keen sense of smell. Most insects are far more sensitive to heat and cold and have a more finely developed tactile sense than human beings; the "feelers" of certain insects respond to the vibrations of objects without coming in contact with the objects themselves.

On the other hand most animals are insensitive to taste, all are incapable of perceiving perspective, and most of them are color blind. Strictly speaking all animals are color blind though some respond to color vibrations through psychic avenues.

There is little need of enlarging upon the phase of the matter since most of us realize that there are different ranges of sensitivity for different species. Furthermore, we understand in a general way that all of our knowledge of the world originates through sense perception. Our sensory organs pick up certain vibrations that emanate from the objects which surround us; then through the magic alchemy of consciousness these vibratory messages are transformed into concepts, or ideas. What we fail to realize is that the world as it *appears* to us is arbitrarily conditioned by the range of our sensitivity.

What we see—what the world looks like, the form of objects in space—is determined for us by two things: (1) the number of sense organs, and (2) their very narrow range of sensitivity.

Certainly the world would appear differently if in addition to the present capacity of our five senses we suddenly acquired the amazing sensitivity of animals and insects. It would be a vaster, more fluid and luminous world. Perhaps the human distinction of day and night would vanish, for we would then "see" as well as felines, night birds, and deep-sea creatures. Much of the world that is now invisible and inaudible would be revealed, giving the impression of a vibrant, living universe.

It is just as certain that the appearance of the world would again change if we were able to transcend the limitations of both human and animal sensitivity. The visible spectrum, for instance, constitutes but a small fraction of sunlight. If we think of a circle of 360 degrees as representing a single ray of light, the visible spectrum is but a very small segment of the circle. What lies beyond in the vast area of light in which we and the beings of the animal world

are wholly insensitive? Science does not know; it is the field
of the radio-ray and the cosmic-ray to be sure, but it is also
an enormous area of unknown mysteries.

Could we transcend the normal limitations of our sense
apparatus we would find ourselves in a luminous world
radiant beyond the capacity of the imagination to conceive.
Not only would there be more light but also new forms of
light and power. New colors would appear and a vibrant,
luminosity would seem to quicken them, giving all colors
the appearance of living forces.

If in addition to this super-sensuous capacity we should
somehow acquire the use of an additional sense—a sixth
sense—even the *form* of objects would change, for the
shape of things in space is also determined by our senses.
In *Tertium Organum,* Ouspensky has shown that the three
dimensions of space which the human intellect is capable of
perceiving—length, width and height—are very elemental;
an infinite universe is multi-dimensional.

The dimensions which we are able to cognize are real
enough, but there is an infinite number of dimensions of
which we are wholly unaware. There is, in addition, to the
three extensions of space with which we are familiar, one
other dimension which we partially apprehend. This fourth
dimension of space is the phenomenon we call time.

Now if time is actually a dimension of space it must
have some of the same qualities exhibited by the other
dimensions, length, width and height. It should enclose a
section of space, binding certain elements into one composite whole. Time does just this; it binds many of our three
dimensional objects and events (people, things, happenings,
days) into such vast cosmic units that we are unable to comprehend them.

The spacial dimensions of length, width and height bind many particles of matter into definite units, or bodies; these are the three dimensional objects with which we are so familiar. Time does the same thing but on a much larger scale—it binds many three dimensional bodies into a cosmic body, many events into a cosmic purpose, many days or years into a cosmic now.

The intellect is incapable of grasping these cosmic wholes. Increased sensitivity of our five sense organs would not enlarge the circumference; it would merely increase our appreciation of the three dimensional world. The quickening of the sixth sense, however, would expand consciousness, thereby revealing a world of four dimensions.

What would the world be like if we suddenly acquired the ability of perceiving all things in their entirety—if we became sensitive to all the vibratory messages of light, of the earth, of the stars, of other human beings—and at the same time acquired the use of one of our latent Soul-senses? The world as we know it would vanish—not theoretically but literally. We would find ourselves in a marvelous four-dimensional world. Consciousness would expand until it seemed to include the universe.

This new universe would enfold all the objects of our old world, but they would be welded into new and startling categories, revealing unimaginable cosmic purposes.

With this vastly expanded consciousness we would be able to contemplate distant points. In reality, our present conception of space would be annihilated; we could "move" freely from one point to another by simply transferring our attention from one point to another.

The "teacup full" of Self-realization would increase until we became conscious of cosmic individuality. We would discover that the personal "I" and the cosmic "I" are in some inexplicable manner one and the same. Perceiving this union we would experience the marvelous realization of eternal life.

We would behold an infinite universe, radiant beyond the power of words to describe. And we would find that the "world" is a living, breathing substance—that it is the mystic thing we call consciousness. The invisible or causal side of life would become visible, revealing its eternal wonders and mysteries.

Ideas would no longer be the media of knowingness. Through the cosmic faculty of intuition we would contain the inner side of all things, discovering indestructible "patterns" which neither require nor admit of explanation. Relative knowledge would thus be replaced by infinite realizations, i.e., by realizations of things in their totality, timeless and changeless.

We would discover also that time, space and motion (or the intellectual concepts about them) are absurd: that time is motionless, that space is both multi-dimensional and dimensionless, and that what we call "change" is the sequential movement of ideas, the process of "thinking."

The illusion of a becoming or changing world would vanish, for it is as unreal as a desert mirage. We would find ourselves immersed in the mystic beauty of a perfected universe which would be realized as Being—a Being which does not evolve since it is infinite, complete, perfect.

5

REALITY ITSELF

RELIGION AFFIRMS THAT the infinite aspect of the universe is spirit. Philosophy affirms that the infiniteness may be found in the fathomless potential of mind. Metaphysics builds its structure of beliefs on the infinitude of love. Science says that the infiniteness of the universe may be found in the indestructible nature of energy. All say about the same thing, using different terms, but none tells us anything of value concerning the underlying reality.

Spirit, mind, love and energy represent something real—something which certainly does exist and which presents itself to our understanding through these four categories—but the reality itself eludes us.

Intellectually we may know a great deal about life, or to state it more accurately we may know how this unknown reality appears to manifest on the three-dimensional plane; but what it is in its essential nature, or how it might manifest itself on a higher plane we do not know.

We begin to approach the truth when we realize that we do not know—when we realize that our intellectual knowledge about life is faulty. This is the first requisite of mystical appreciation, and the very attitude of mind which makes intuitive perception possible.

If we accept the premise of an infinite universe we must likewise accept it as an unknown universe, the mystery of which we long to apprehend. The Soul then becomes a powerful magnet, lifting us slowly but surely above the dark realm of consciousness which is ruled by reason.

What we know, or think we know about life, must be set aside; it must be recognized as illusory knowledge. That which we desire to know, and for which we must be willing to make any sacrifice, is beyond imaginative conception. Therefore it will have to make itself known through some avenue other than the intellect, and until illumination occurs it must appear to us as the unknown.

Let us call this unknown element *reality*, meaning that which actually exists as distinguished from our concepts and ideas about it which may be wholly imaginary and fictitious—rather, which must be imaginary and fictitious since the reality is infinite.

Spirit, mind, love, energy then become names; they are merely "tags" which we use to indicate certain characteristics of an unknown magnitude or person. We know how these several characteristics appear to beings like ourselves. What the underlying reality might be like is the ever-intriguing mystery.

It is not a simple and easy transition. Much as we would like to believe that our knowledge of the world is correct as far as it goes, and that we will gradually learn more about life through the tireless efforts of our scientists and philosophers, we must disabuse our minds of this basic error. At least we must do so if we would "know the truth which will set us free." For our knowledge of the world does not pertain to an infinite universe; it pertains to an imaginary, finite world which has no real existence—rather, which exists only in the minds of human beings and which owes its existence to the peculiar limitations of our sensory equipment.

Classical science knows nothing whatever about the real universe (the infinite magnitude). This means not only that science is unable to determine the fundamental nature of its "energy," but also that all scientific hypotheses are formulated from the finite evidence of incomplete sense perception. The microscope and telescope are indeed marvelous inventions, but they simply extend our mental vision; they do not expand consciousness.

Our scientific knowledge of the world as it appears to be is useful. Our knowledge of the manner in which universal forces appear to operate is also useful. Such knowledge permits us to invent and make use of machines, to forecast the weather, produce better crops, paint pictures, print books, alleviate pain, etc. All of these things help to make existence more tolerable and we should enjoy them as fully as possible. But no scientific hypothesis yet devised, nor all of them combined, will lead us to reality.

If we are sincere in our quest we must learn to distinguish between this kind of knowledge (regardless of its scientific authenticity or academic approbation) and the mystic knowledge of the Soul. For so long as we permit ourselves to be deceived by the former we remain insensitive to the Soul-faculty which alone can reveal an infinite universe.

6

FREE WILL AND PURPOSE

IT IS DIFFICULT to comprehend the vast differences between these two forms of knowledge—the knowledge of the mind and the knowledge of the Soul—yet there are a few fundamental distinctions which will help to bridge the gap in our understanding of the mystic thing we call consciousness.

(1) Concepts or ideas are peculiar to our present form of consciousness. They are "particles" of consciousness in much the same sense that atoms are particles of matter; they are the fragmentary units of consciousness the motion of which is called thought. But ideas, being finite, cannot be the units of consciousness in the realm of the Soul. Cosmic or Soul-consciousness is not a thinking or reasoning state; it is a form of intellection which deals with infinite realizations—vast four-dimensional patterns and categories. To carry the analogy of the atom a bit further we might say that one of these categories would be similar to a human body which is composed of billions of atoms, integrated in such a manner that the identity of the atoms is lost. Just as we do not think of ourselves in terms of atoms but in terms of human beings, so will the units of mentation change when we achieve Cosmic Consciousness.

(2) Realizing this we see that our logic, being the logic of relative ideas or "atoms," would not apply in the realm of the Soul. Rational discrimination, the comparison and

31

contrasting of finite ideas, would be impossible in a realm of consciousness where ideas are not even recognized. Reasonable as our logic appears to us it is meaningless, even ridiculous, from the standpoint of the Soul.

Conversely this implies that cosmic logic, which is the logic of unities, would likewise appear contradictory and meaningless to the intellectual, could it be formulated and stated in words. For example, there is a difference between good and evil according to our logic. We say these things are opposites; our conception of them as opposites enables us to contrast, distinguish and define them. And consciously or unconsciously we classify all experiences as good or evil (pleasant or painful).

The Soul makes no such distinction. In the realm of Cosmic Consciousness there cannot be a conception of opposing forces, for the first demand of infiniteness is a realization of unity. All of one's experiences are bound together as an immense body of experience, welded into a great four-dimensional pattern by the real but invisible line of time. The four-dimensional pattern has cosmic significance and purpose which are incomprehensible to us at present, but the innumerable experiences and realizations of which it is composed are neither good nor evil. They are necessary. Thus if we attempt to state the nature of things from the standpoint of the Soul we will be compelled to say that good and evil are one in their purpose, or else we must say that good and evil as such do not exist.

(3) The Soul is ever conscious of existence, of continuous being. It realizes life as an ocean of vital substance in which it is immersed and from which there is no escape. The incidents of birth and death, phenomenal realities to the intellect do not alter the Soul's realization of eternal and unbroken existence. Extinction is therefore an absurdity.

Real and logical as death appears to us, conscious union with the Soul will reveal the error of our thinking. Should we attempt to express the realization of eternal existence, our statements would of necessity be counter-rational and therefore meaningless to the intellect. We might say as one great mystic has already said "I am *that* I AM," but from the standpoint of human logic, separate existence, conditioned by birth and death, is the reality.

(4) In the realm of cosmic verities past and future are realities, for the multitude of events which constitutes our "days" represents a four-dimensional section of space. This is not entirely beyond our comprehension. We know that numerous kinds of materials are required for the building of a house. We must have lumber of different dimensions and grades, shingles, nails, screws, plaster, cement, hardware, glass, paint, paper, tile, metals of various kinds in the form of plumbing and heating fixtures, and a host of other items. Each of these items is distinctive, each has its own characteristic shape and purpose. What becomes of these items—do they cease to exist when the workmen fit them into their proper places? No, each item continues to exist and to function, but all of them are welded into a much larger unit which occupies a vastly larger section of space.

Our days and their innumerable events may be likened to the materials which enter into the construction of a house. These diverse materials are unified in vast four-dimensional patterns, but we are unable to perceive the cosmic realities since they occupy four-dimensional space.

Our perception of these patterns is piecemeal, thus it appears to us that there is a movement in time. A blind person with but four active senses, would be compelled to examine any large object with the fingertips and it would disclose its shape and proportions little by little. Never would it reveal the phenomena of perspective and color, nor the ever-changing effects of light and shadow. Some of the most important characteristics of objects, especially proximity to other objects and their relationships and unities, would be unobserved. Nevertheless, the blind are able to discover the shape of things in space.

Should a blind man repossess the fifth sense, the laborious examination of objects would be unnecessary. Instead of piece-by-piece perception he would see the building or tree in its three-dimensional entirety. He would also discover unsuspected beauties and unities, and thereby gain a new realization of natural purposes.

Our intellectual perception of four-dimensional objects is analogous. It is slow and laborious, little by little, and unaware that we are dealing with objects of a section of space which is invisible to us, we say there is a succession of days, a movement of time. Should we gain the use of a sixth sense our mental blindness would disappear. We would suddenly realize that the real world is not invisible, but that lack of spiritual sight made the world seem dark. Now we would see the larger patterns and apprehend something of their amazing portent.

In order to express the relationships of the cosmic order we would say that the phenomenon which we now call time is a force which encloses a section of four-dimensional space, which space is revealed to the intellect little by little, thus producing the illusion of motion. This motion ceases when we achieve the larger perspective, for we then see groups of objects and events in their entirety.

Further, a new time-sense arises in consciousness and its chief characteristic is its immobility. In other words cosmic time is realized as a dimensionless now. In terms of Soul logic then, we would have to say that there is neither time nor motion, that there is neither past nor future, but that all things now exist in their cosmic completeness. Or to state differently, past and future are existing realities—they exist spatially and are therefore eternal.

(5) According to our logic we have free will. On that point certain philosophies and theology agree. Free will, however, is impossible in an infinite universe; it is just as impossible as separate existence. The reality is indicated by the very term, universe. The world is *one,* and there is but *one* will.

This is unquestionably the most difficult aspect of the subject for us to grasp, and there are two main obstacles which make it so. First, we cherish the belief of free will; personal autonomy is our most loved possession; in relinquishing the very human belief it seems to us that we are surrendering our lives. Second, we do not differentiate clearly enough between "will" and "purpose."

Let us consider the second obstacle first. Generally speaking the term "will" connotes a coercive force, while the word "purpose" means the object or result at which something is aimed. It is true that in our lives we must often use a coercive force in order to achieve our ends, but this does not apply in the realm of the Soul. Cosmic life has but one purpose and that is to live, to express its livingness. It expresses itself through all instruments and in an infinite variety of ways. The only kind of coercion possible is that which is made known to us in the form of desire—the urge to live fully in all departments of our being.

"God's will for man" is no different in this respect than is God's will for the earth, for plants, for animals. It does not follow, however, that our lives are unplanned and that we can express life fully by uncoordinated emotional activity. Man is a more complicated and expressive instrument than that, now. Still it is not man's intellect that does the planning; cosmic patterns of action already exist and the Soul is the architect; it is these patterns which unfold for us from day to day, from moment to moment.

On the surface this might seem to imply fatalism. If we mean by fatalism an inescapable destiny the assumption is true enough; but if we mean a destiny imposed by mechanical forces the implication is erroneous. It is the Soul which determines the individual's destiny—that side of our being which is ever immersed in the radiance of cosmic wisdom.

In regard to the first obstacle, the desire to retain personal autonomy, it must be said that our logic requires us to hold fast to this belief. It seems that we are separate individuals, opposed by other self-seeking individuals and an unfriendly world. It also appears that reason and the personal will are the highest faculties of being; should we relinquish reason and the will we would be lost.

In reality there is a true course for every individual and it is determined by the Soul. How well or how quickly we learn to apprehend our own course—which now exists as a four-dimensional pattern—depends on how sensitive we become to our intuitive faculties.

These four-dimensional patterns can best be described by the word, "purpose." Viewed in their entirety the materials of which they are composed—the events and relationships and experiences of rational existence—are obscured; only the great cosmic purpose is apparent.

From the standpoint of the Soul there is no concern about the manner in which these cosmic objectives will be achieved, nor is there any need for hurry; because they are cosmic they will be fulfilled. Yet there are infinite possibilities in every moment, many ways of accomplishing the same end. The short-cuts are always counter-rational. Thus the more sensitive we become to the intuitive promptings of the Soul the easier will our progress be.

The Soul's purposes will be achieved regardless of the costs in mental and physical suffering, but this does not mean that pain and loss and disappointment are inescapable. As indicated previously it depends upon the integration of being. Conscious union with the Soul is the great and immediate purpose, and every effort we make to achieve this mystical unity emancipates us in some degree from the world of opposites.

We reason that one and one make two, that two and two make four, etc. But in Cosmic Consciousness there is no realization of diversity. There is *one*, indivisible except through the prism of the intellect. Thus from the cosmic standpoint we are compelled to say that each one is the whole, or that the infinite universe is contained within the Soul.

7

Releasing the Intellect

From an intellectual standpoint the logic of the Soul is certainly illogical. We are quite sure that the world is one thing and that we are something else. We know there is diversity and multiplicity. We are just as certain about the reality of good and evil, birth and death, and all other pairs of opposites. And try as we will we cannot escape the pressure of a swiftly moving time, nor can we shatter the illusion of external motion.

This cannot be denied, but neither can it be denied that we view the world "through a glass darkly." Our limited senses and the faculty of reason constitute the prism which produces the illusions of diversity, motion, death.

It is a simple matter for us to reason that the intellect is a perfect instrument when rightly employed. This is the basic tenet of the Socratic philosophy and it is not without virtue. But, as this great master of logic pointed out, the intellect is the cause of our spiritual blindness, and if we would discover truth (or as he calls it, the "right") we are sooner or later forced to abandon logic. Reason can carry us into abstract realms of thought but it cannot bridge the chasm which separates the real and the unreal.

Were the universe actually finite then the finite conclusions of our logic would be valid; but if the universe is infinite it will also be illogical, non-relative, unitary, and therefore incomprehensible to the intellect. Intellectually we shall never be able to apprehend truth since it is infinite.

Our logic is useful up to a certain point in our development, and the "light of reason" is enthroned as a god. For the men and women who are still struggling upward from the mire of emotional consciousness, this is as it should be, for reason is the feeble light which guides us through the intricate and confusing paths of the three-dimensional world.

Reason, however, is not the light which leads us beyond this world. Having achieved self-consciousness a new, though dimmer, light is offered, which, if followed, will guide us unerringly into an altogether different realm of consciousness where self-awareness gives place to Soul-awareness. The new light is faith.

Faith in what? Certainly not the things we have learned to believe in—the rational conclusions of the intellect. Faith in an infinite, super-rational universe—a universe which reveals itself to us as Soul, or Being.

Let us not misinterpret the above statement. Humanity has always believed in and worshiped a supreme being, and at the same time has gone about its business believing in the reality of a three-dimensional world. It is this dual attitude which binds humanity to the treadmill of illusory existence. If we are to achieve emancipation we must choose the light of the Soul; we cannot follow both, for the paths diverge. The light of reason leads to intellectualism, the cold region of "outer darkness," with its inevitable conflict of opinion and realization of death. The light of faith leads to a realm of unimaginable radiance, the realization of unity and timeless existence.

The light of faith leads us away from reason, toward the realization of a mystic and unknown universe—an infinite cosmos. It leads us away from creeds, philosophies, and the scientific dogma of the modem intellectual world.

If we follow the new light we must somehow transcend logical thinking and the traditional beliefs regarding the naturalness of the three-dimensional world: We must learn to stretch the mind in an attempt to grasp the illogical, the super-natural, contradictory and meaningless as it first appears. Let us remember that the so-called natural world is, in reality, unnatural since it is but a thin distorted image of an infinite universe. What we call the natural world is simply the familiar world; the natural world is infinite.

Let us not be deceived by the affirmations of science that "little by little the unknown is being resolved." Our scientific investigation of the world reveals nothing except the prismatic distortions of the intellect. Intriguing and useful as such knowledge may be, it is not true knowledge. The scientist is blinded by the same mental astigmatism which affects all mankind; he perceives multiplicity and diversity, the three-dimensional shape of objects in space, the illusory movement of time, and believes they are real. Upon this platform of false sense-evidence he builds a structure of rational dogma which must continually be altered, and which is now so patched and leaky that it appears to be falling apart.

Science and philosophy, and in many instances theology, endeavor to make the world appear logical. Such is the province of the intellect. We must all pass through the elementary stages of self-consciousness, believing in separate existence and the reality of opposites. But we must also pass beyond the logic of duality, seeking a realization of oneness.

Accurate as our scientific knowledge is, and useful as it is in the "production, construction, and protection of property," as Plato affirmed, we must try to realize that it does not represent the real. Our type of knowledge permits us to live rational lives, to become mechanical robots in a mechanical world, to wage wars for the establishment of peace, to destroy surpluses in order to make prosperity, to permit starvation in the midst of plenty, but it will never take us beyond such absurdities. These things—war and peace, famine and plenty, sickness and health, birth and death—are inherent in reason itself. And just as long as there is a rational humanity the conflict of opposites will persist.

We cannot overcome the existence of opposites by learning to reason more accurately, for our logic depends on the conception of opposites. But let us destroy the ascendancy of reason, i.e., remove reason from the throne it has occupied so long, and the world of opposites will begin to disintegrate.

As I have already intimated this is a difficult task and at times it is very painful. Reason will battle for its supremacy and time and again it will regain its throne, just as instinct and emotion once fought and won engagements when their supremacy was threatened. But once we begin, determined to wage a relentless war against the forces of intellectual darkness, victory is certain. For back of such determination is the mighty cosmic power of the Soul, guiding us through the abysmal darkness which ensues when we dethrone the "light of reason."

How long will it take to achieve cosmic illumination? No one can say. It may require a month or a lifetime, but once we have set our feet on the "straight and narrow path" there is no turning backward. Having pierced the flimsy garb of thought and discovered its immature and misshapen forms, having discovered that reason has never led us beyond ephemeral and transitory beliefs, we will continue in the search for reality regardless of the costs.

And we shall arrive. Someday when it is least expected the veil of nescience will be rolled away, disclosing a world of stupendous radiance vibrant with living colors, overflowing with harmonious power. In the light of this cosmic splendor we will discover the profound and simple secrets of life, the meaning and purpose of all created things, the cause and extent of our being. All questions of the intellect will be answered as we bathe in the infinite wisdom of the Soul, and the ecstasy of reunion will lift us to speechless, unimaginable heights of super-sensuous joy.

This is the freedom, the joy, the worship or adoration, the peace, the realization of completeness, held forth in the teachings of the avatars; and of which all human concepts and emotions are merely symbolic, the empty husks of our world of darkness. And the real is not to be experienced in some other existence or upon some other plane. We now live in an infinite universe and there are closed doors which we must open.

This then, a higher form of consciousness which reveals the infinite, is the mysterious goal toward which we are ever impelled. Until we have achieved this unity of consciousness we cannot know the meaning of peace, nor can we experience wholeness and perfection, for that which we discover is the Self, the one eternal person which broods in the heart of every human being. It is the alter ego, the Soul—that part of our being which includes the infinite cosmos—and of which we must become conscious if we would experience wholeness.

PART TWO

THE QUEST FOR REALITY

8

THE PREPARATION

WE MAY RIGHTFULLY ASK, how can Reality be known? If we cannot know it through the instrumentality of a finite intellect, then how can it be contacted and known?

It seems to us that we have but one knowing instrument, the mind, and that if we are to know anything we must know it mentally. In other words we believe that consciousness depends upon the functioning of the intellectual faculties, and that ideas and emotions are the only media of knowingness.

It is true that the intellectual faculties limit us to conceptual knowledge, i.e., the realization of ideas and their relationships. Beyond this the mind cannot go. Whenever we try to imagine a limitless space, or eternity, we find that we cannot do so. Pushing the imaginary limits of space out in an ever-widening circle we at length reach a point where the mind is numbed by the stupendous task and hastily seeks to regain its equilibrium. But regardless of how far we succeed in pushing back the limits of space our realization is always limited by the imaginary circle and is therefore finite.

The same thing happens when we attempt to realize an eternal now. Somewhere, it seems, there must have been a beginning, and somewhere along the line there must be an end. Intellectually we cannot realize time as a motionless now; we cannot strip it of the "before" and "after."

If the intellect were our only knowing instrument we would thereby be condemned to perpetual darkness, for the world in which we "live, move and have our being" is infinite. The intellect, however, is not the only instrument available. We have cosmic faculties. They are as fundamentally a part of our being as the physical senses. Through them the world is not strained, but is perceived directly and in its totality.

How are these faculties quickened, and how is the transition from a finite to an infinite form of consciousness effected? What are the specific requirements for initiation? What is the experience like and why is there so little information about it?

In a rather general way I have attempted to answer these and similar questions in Part One. But I realize that generalities are not very satisfying. We want specific details.

There is in existence today a great deal of information regarding the fourth dimension, or as we have previously termed it, Soul-consciousness, but much of it is unintelligible to the modem mind. There is as yet no language of the Soul, for the "categories" and "patterns" of the higher consciousness are not only unnamed but unnameable. In an effort to express the meaning of infinite magnitudes most writers have resorted to symbolism or allegory. Some have created terminologies which are without meaning today. Ezekiel, for example, and John the Divine have but one theme—Cosmic Consciousness—but their writings have little significance for the exacting, scientific mind.

Thus it is that in the following pages I tell of my own experience in the quest for reality; of the painful process of disillusionment; the sudden and unexpected discovery of a new world and a few of its amazing revelations; the subsequent realization of the unvarying requisites for initiation into the world of infinite magnitudes.

Out of necessity the narrative is told in the first person singular, and the pronoun "I" appears all too frequently. But in spite of this obvious defect it was written from a very detached, impersonal standpoint. A great deal of mental and emotional dissection was needed, a relentless probing for the basic motives and attitudes of mind which make the transition to a higher form of consciousness possible.

I frankly admit that in many ways I was unprepared for what happened. I had had no esoteric training of any kind, I was extremely self-centered and in one sense of the word very materialistic. All this I try to make clear in the opening paragraphs. Still I was endowed with a capacity which is sometimes a virtue: I was unconventionally direct, single-minded; once a course of action was determined all bridges were burned behind me; my natural inclination was to keep on moving, regardless of the consequences.

In this, the most adventurous of all quests, a singleness of purpose brought me quickly to the threshold of a new world. Once I discovered that there is a difference between intellectual knowledge and Reality I was ruthless in my attempts to destroy my beliefs in the validity of factual knowledge. I had no idea of my destination, no knowledge whatever of a vaster world which lies just beyond the limits of rational consciousness. Guided only by the tormenting desire for truth, I sought to destroy all that was not truth. By such methods I achieved the emancipation which made initiation possible.

While temperaments differ there is but one way in which human beings may discover Truth, or Reality, or God, or whatever we choose to call the underlying "source of being."

By this I do not mean that our experiences will be the same; rather, that there are certain principles involved, both psychological and religious, which govern the transition, and if the demands of these principles are met the resultant effect will be the same. In short, Reality is changeless, and because it is not apprehended through the intellect but through faculties which do not permit distortion, the great experience will be the same for all men and women, regardless of temperament or the nature of personal experiences.

While it is not within my power to describe this experience so as to convey more than a vague impression of its grandeur, mystery, ecstasy, and freedom, I have tried to do so. It is impossible, for instance, to describe the realization of timeless existence, or to express the realization of a living universe in which all things are alive and conscious, even those inorganic forms which we consider lifeless and insentient.

It is fully as difficult to paint a picture of a perfected, non-evolving universe in which opposites do not exist, as to describe the radiant splendor of a form of consciousness in which it is possible to commune with all things without resorting to cumbersome thoughts, or of describing the vast freedom and incredible realizations of peace, power and completeness. It is vastly more difficult to express the new relationship, for one remains an individual and at the same time becomes the universe.

The difficulty arises because we cannot reduce infinite realizations to finite concepts without losing Reality. This is exactly what the intellect does now, and this is why we must abandon the intellect as a knowing instrument if we would discover the real nature of the world we live in—which is a *Being*, rather than a lifeless, *becoming* force.

This narrative, therefore, will tell us very little about the real, but it may disclose a great deal regarding the secret path by which emancipation is achieved.

9

THE PRELUDE

FOR YEARS, HOW MANY I do not remember, I had been searching for some kind of "reality." What this reality might consist of I did not know, but I knew what it could not be: It could not be a *belief* in something. Many disillusioning experiences had shown me that all human beliefs are chimerical. Reality, if there were such a thing, would have to reveal itself as something wholly independent of one's beliefs.

I think most mature men and women realize the chimerical nature of beliefs. We know that our personal beliefs about the world, self, others, are always in a state of flux; that our views about life have been changing since infancy; that without peradventure tomorrow's beliefs will be different from today's. What we do not realize is that we have nothing except beliefs. Our individual worlds are made up of personal beliefs about things; we have opinions concerning everything under the sun, but the things themselves are unknown.

We have opinions about the sun and the moon and all the rest of the solar system, and some regarding the stellar universe. Your opinions may conform to one scientific hypothesis, mine to another. But neither you nor I, nor any scientist nor group of scientists, knows much that is positive about the moon, to say nothing about the planets and the stars. Our knowledge is derived from inference, and the so-called facts about the universe are nothing more than rational conclusions. We can construct, destroy, believe or disbelieve these rational conclusions as we choose.

Generally speaking we accept facts as truth, and say that our beliefs represent Reality. They do not, of course. Beliefs are always changing whereas to be real a thing would of necessity have to be changeless, non-relative, absolute.

At least this was the kind of reality for which I had been searching. We say that God is such a Reality—that the creative power is changeless and absolute. I was willing to concede that this might be so, but how was one to know? How could one know there *is* a supreme being? Only by inference, apparently.

However, I had reached a point where it was impossible for me to accept inferential knowledge as truth. One could twist such knowledge into the most fantastic beliefs, and then without realizing it accept these fantastic beliefs as truth. The more I examined my beliefs the more certain I became that the whole structure was illusory—that the most reasonable scientific hypothesis was just as faulty as the superstitions acquired during childhood.

I do not recall how or when this realization began to dawn, but it seems to me now that since my earliest years I had mistrusted all knowledge except that gained through personal experience. As a child I had little interest in academic studies and it was only with great patience that my parents managed to keep me in school. Experience was my god, and anything which called for physical skill or ingenuity offered a challenge which I could not resist. Having a strong, well-knit body, a capacity for hard work, and an overwhelming desire to try everything once, my youth was not without adventure.

Shortly after my twenty-first birthday America entered World War I, and I enlisted at once. But during the five short years preceding the war I lived a strenuous and wonderful life. Beside attending school somewhat irregularly I had traveled thousands of miles on my own, knew many great cities almost as intimately as my home town, had trouped with carnivals and circuses, worked in factories and harvest fields, in drug, grocery and department stores, in the advertising department of a street railway company, had tried specialty selling, construction work, restaurant work. I had also been advance agent for a national lecturer, managed concessions in an amusement park, worked on the Mississippi River, and had played part of a season with a world famous concert band.

All of these experiences were short-lived, for I wanted only the thrill of excitement and achievement. As soon as I had tested my capacity and absorbed sufficient knowledge to make me feel somewhat "experienced" I was ready for new fields.

I made few friends and many enemies for my egotism and enthusiasm were practically boundless. On the whole I had a high disregard for normal existence, for theories, for the opinions of those whose experiences were more limited than my own. Reality, it seemed to me, could be known in but one way and that way was through personal experience.

My desire for all sorts of experiences was so great and so genuine that I drew no line of distinction between those usually considered desirable and those considered not desirable. I found fully as much satisfaction in riding the rods of a freight train as riding the cushions of a Pullman. The hobo "jungles" were just as fascinating as the dining rooms of the great hotels. Pacific Street in San Francisco and Washington Alley in St. Louis held as much attraction for me as the boulevards. And the men and women of the amusement world and the "under-world" were just as human, and in their way just as honest, as the men and women who spent their lives and money "up-town."

During the war some subtle change was wrought in my viewpoint. I did not know it at the time nor am I sure now what took place nor how it happened. I did not come to disbelieve in the value of personal experience exactly, but I began to wonder why one wanted experience. It may have been the result of regimentation—the realization that I was simply a cog in a vast machine. Perhaps it resulted from the realization that human life is the cheapest of all commodities—that one's personal existence is not only uncertain but unimportant.

At any rate two years' service overseas shattered my egocentric illusion of Reality. Shattered may be too strong a word, but my former conviction of "rightness" had begun to crumble. The capacity for impulsive action had begun to diminish and I became more cautious. I tried to reason things out in advance, to estimate the costs and forecast the probable results of my actions. This, it seemed to me now, was a more intelligent way of life.

Perhaps money, property, substantial citizenship were the things worth seeking; and perhaps the desire for new experiences and the great freedom I had enjoyed before the war were simply the expressions of my immaturity. At least the possession of money and property offered a new hope: They might give me the sense of personal "rightness" and security I had lost. So for a number of years I pursued these things earnestly and with some success.

During the first years of the Depression, along with millions of others, I learned that material possessions do not bring security, and that a single wave of fear can wipe out the results of years of labor and sacrifice. As the old order crumbled I began to grasp blindly at straws. Will-power, it seemed to me now, was the thing most needed. It was real—a personal quality which depressions could not lick. So I clung rather desperately to this straw, slowly building a stronger will through various methods of physical and mental discipline. For the first time in my life I took an interest in books, reading everything I could find on the culture of will-power. I applied myself heart and Soul, and in accord with the new philosophy I predetermined what I would do, what I would be, and what I would get from life.

It took two long, grim years to discover that the personal will is an impotent force when pitted against the imagination and the forces of destiny; and that if a man wills to do or be something which is contrary to his inmost nature he cannot succeed. Taking the exponents of will-culture at their word, and believing that all forces in the universe yield to the will of man, I had set a most desirable goal for myself but it was one for which I had no special aptitude. Will-power alone was not sufficient; it could not make a square peg fit into a round hole.

During these years, however, I developed a thirst for knowledge and a great respect for logical reasoning. My parents had succeeded in getting me through preparatory school and I had had one year of college work, but I had not been intrigued by academic studies. Now I perceived the advantages of an education. Here was something real. Knowledge was the one thing which gave one power over the world and his fellowmen.

I plunged into the study of psychology, history, physiology, philosophy, and so avid was my thirst for knowledge that for more than two years I read a book a day—the dusty tomes of ancient thinkers as well as the works of contemporary writers. I assimilated a rather large amount of factual knowledge, but eventually became confused by the conflict of opinions. Each writer offered his own personal opinions regarding the subject discussed, and always substantiated it with logical or scientific proof, but too often these profound conclusions were diametrically opposed. I began to realize that nothing can be known with absolute certainty, and that the best I could hope for was a broader basis for my own opinions.

Out of this maze of indiscriminate reading one conclusion was forced upon me which caused me a great deal of trouble, namely, that there is no reason whatever for believing our civilization is permanent. Empires bloom and die with almost clock-like regularity. Grecian, Roman, Carthaginian, Babylonian, Syrian, Chaldean, Incan, Tiajurian, and many others—some as great or greater than our own—appeared out of nowhere only to fade into the same nothingness.

Why do civilizations come and go like this? And why do we ignore this obvious fact and assume that our own civilization will endure? Why do we deceive ourselves into believing that there is anything real or permanent in our way of life?

I could not answer these questions nor could I find any writer, ancient or modem, who could answer them for me. True, many men had opinions to offer—theories of cosmogony which ranged from the strictest kind of materialism to the hysteria of psychic phenomena.

It was simple enough to reason that each writer had caught a glimpse of the truth, divergent as their views seemed to be. But in attempting to absorb the true ideas I realized that I was getting exactly nowhere as far as truth itself was concerned. The net result of my efforts was nothing but a synthetic product, a substitute for Reality which left me as hungry as before. I wanted something more substantial—a conviction of Reality which would leave no room for doubt.

In desperation I finally turned to religion and for a time believed that I was upon solid ground. This was indeed a tremendous step, for in spite of my early training I had become thoroughly materialistic and sincerely agnostic. I believed in the scientific doctrine of a mechanistic universe, and with the scientific fraternity looked upon all religious beliefs as outmoded.

Eventually I found myself adrift in a senseless world in which all men and women were as lost as I was. Yet there was a difference; I knew I was lost, while the men and women who constructed the theories and wrote the books did not realize their predicament. They believed in a theory, or an imaginative belief, nothing more. This I could not do. There was not one thing to which I could cling with any sincerity. There was a terrible loneliness in my heart, an intense desire for knowledge of Reality, I cared not what the nature of the Reality might be. This demand became so imperative that I realized I could not go on indefinitely; either I must find something real to which I could anchor or I would certainly lose my sanity.

It was not that I found no virtue in the practices of philosophy and religion. The teachings of the great philosophers and messiahs were workable and paid real dividends. But I was not searching for dividends, either moral or material.

I wanted to know the meaning and purpose of the created universe, why I was here, where I was going, and I could not accept second-hand theories or doctrines. I had examined hundreds of them and found them to be nothing but the rational conclusions of men and women who were speculating about Reality, and while their speculations might be interesting they could not be true.

10

THE ABYSS

ONE NIGHT, HIGH IN THE SIERRAS where I was camped for the summer, I gave the solution up as hopeless. Numbed by the mental effort of trying to make sense out of a senseless confusion I lay quiescent, lost in a silent contemplation of the stars. I do not know how long I rested in this thoughtless state, but suddenly I heard a voice, strong and steady: "Be not afraid; you are my son!"

I started up from my cot, thinking someone had approached my isolated camp, yet in the same instant I knew the words had sounded within my own being. The words were audible, as clearly objective as any I had ever heard, yet I knew they were spoken inwardly by some "voice" apart from my own consciousness. There was a mystery about it that gave me a tingling sense of awe. I knew something had spoken to me, a something greater than myself, and at that moment the phenomenon appeared far more important than the message. In my excitement, or rather exultation, I had gotten up from the cot and was wandering around the camp, but I returned, thinking the voice might speak again. Hours of silence, of expectant waiting and listening brought no other word.

In the light of day, with nature busy around me, the mystery of the voice began to diminish. I reasoned that my subjective mind had merely adopted this means of satisfying a deep desire. Yet the solution did not fully convince me.

There had been a serene sense of power behind the voice, a calmness which conveyed an impression of superior wisdom. I could not associate these things with my understanding of the subjective mind.

But why, I asked myself, were the words so scriptural? Again my only solution was the subjective mind; it had used words similar to those which had occupied my attention during the past months. But the more I reasoned against the possibility of a voice apart from my own consciousness the more certain I became of the opposite. Something about the voice itself defied all my efforts to make it appear as an illusion.

I spent many hours of the days and nights listening inwardly, stilling my thoughts in an attempt to achieve the same passivity which, I believed, had given rise to the mystical experience. But I did not hear it again that summer nor have I ever heard it since. However, during the days which followed I began to experience revelations of the most illuminating nature. Familiar scriptural passages declared their secrets to me, revealing inexplicable meanings. These illuminations came quite suddenly and at odd moments, quite often while I tramped or fished, or while my mind and hands were busy with the camp chores. These illuminations were an exhilarating experience, for they came so suddenly and of their own volition. Whence they came I had not the slightest idea, but of one thing I was thoroughly convinced: The source of this inward light was superior to my intellect.

Meanings which I could not comprehend intellectually at all were revealed in a quick flash of light which seemed to illuminate my consciousness without involving a process of rational thought.

As nearly as I can recollect, these illuminations continued to come intermittently for several weeks, becoming less frequent with the passing days. By the time I returned to the city they had ceased coming altogether. The business of making a living soon engrossed me and for a little while life was quite normal.

The respite was short lived. Everything I tried to do was wrong, every decision led to more difficulties. Again I began questioning the unknown. Why all this struggle for survival? Why should helpless men and women be thrown into an arena which they could not control? Why should millions of men and women stand in bread-lines day after day trying to prolong an existence which had no meaning? Such questions bothered many people, I know, for we had reached the bottom of the Great Depression, but I demanded answers to these queries. It was the same old quest for reality in a new guise.

One day I had to make a trip up-country to conclude an unpleasant piece of business, the surrender of legal ownership to the last piece of property we owned. Strangely enough I felt much lighter after signing the deed. For the first time in weeks I felt free. Returning to the city over an old, almost deserted highway, I began musing over the mystery of the voice which had spoken to me in the mountains, and again fell into the same peaceful state of mind. This time there was no voice but quite suddenly I saw the world with its multitudes of men and women outlined against the blue afternoon sky. The men and women seemed to be struggling in an opaque mist which hovered about them, but of which they were entirely unconscious. Each person, it seemed, was bent upon selfish ends and unaware of any guiding force other than his or her own desires. Yet from each individual there extended upward lines of force, or invisible cords, to a 'something higher.'

The 'something higher' I could not discern but I knew it was there. The lines of force I could see clearly though I realized that the people could not see them. These lines controlled the actions of men and women, or rather they were the avenues by which the higher intelligence controlled the lives of men and women. Vaguely I sensed that individuals are greater than they know; that there is an undiscovered something above or beyond the limits of human perception.

It lasted but an instant, but as in the case of the voice it carried its own conviction. There was one difference: The voice was real, but I realized that what I had just seen was a vision, that it was symbolical rather than real. But I was convinced of a hidden import which, as nearly as it lends itself to interpretation, is that no man or woman is lost or alone; that each, as he or she knows self, is but a fragmentary part of a 'greater self.'

I do not know how much time elapsed between the appearance of this vision and the strange and wonderful experience which followed. It was not long, perhaps a few months. But I do recall something of the state of mind which immediately preceded it. Due to these recent experiences it would seem that my thirst for reality might have been tempered but such was not the case. These things satisfied my longings only for an instant; they were as single drops of moisture to a man dying of thirst. They tantalized and spurred me on instead of giving me respite.

I had arrived at a point where it was impossible for me to trust either my reason or my senses. For a long time I had been aware of the utter unreliability of sense perception, but now I realized that the faculty of reason is no more trustworthy than the sense organs.

Every rational conclusion could be successfully contradicted by reasoning from a different standpoint. Day after day I applied this principle in my thinking: I reasoned both for and against every proposition which presented itself, taking one side as dispassionately as the other. Nothing, it seemed, is either true or false; everything is a matter of belief. Whatever one believes is true for the moment; it is true for the one who believes it and remains true until a different belief is accepted.

It began to appear that God, as a reality or as something apart from human belief, did not exist at all. God was an invention of the human imagination as many scientists affirmed, for He could be reasoned into existence or out of existence at will. And the arguments for non-existence were just as substantial as those for the existence of a deity.

At length I began to doubt my own existence. Logically I could disprove it, for according to the accepted scientific theory man is a product of physio-magnetic forces, and intelligence is merely a by-product of this mechanical action. Thus the concept "I" is a transient illusion; it is merely a "thought" which is dispersed upon disintegration of the body. Being non-existent before birth and non-existent after death the human Soul is a fantasy of the imagination; nothing actually exists except the mechanical energy of the universe.

One day it occurred to me that it was within my power to change this condition and thereby prove or disprove the reality of existence. By simply inhaling a little carbon monoxide gas I could find out whether I was real—whether personal existence continued after death. It was a tempting idea and one which recurred more or less persistently. But it was too great a risk. As long as I lived there was a possibility of discovering Reality; extinction would preclude such a possibility. I felt that if there were some Reality—a something beyond reason which could not be thought into existence or out of existence—that I would gladly give my life for one convincing taste of it: I would gladly accept annihilation if only I might be convinced of its existence first.

Out of this chaos came the realization that the whole world was an illusion. There was no positive proof of anything, not even personal existence. Every scientific theory could be disproved, in fact some of them were always being disproved. Einstein's theory had destroyed many time-honored scientific beliefs. Given a little more time some other new theory would displace the theory of relativity and its satellites. It was an endless game which was very fascinating but which got us exactly nowhere.

This violent emotional reaction against reason, logical beliefs, relative knowledge, brought me to what appeared to be the end of the world. I had reached a point beyond which there was nothing. Many nights I lay sleepless, poised on the brink of a bottomless void trying desperately to find a new foothold. Into this darkness I sometimes plunged as in a nightmare, falling for eons of time. The despairing realization that there was nothing left to live for, and perhaps nothing beyond was more excruciating than any pain or loss I had ever known. I knew but one prayer and that was for light.

These moments of darkness and pain were not continuous. They came at intervals over a period of several weeks, but seemed to grow in intensity with every recurrence. I went about my work from force of habit and necessity and I think with a faint hope that my prayer might someday be answered. It was a lonely battle, for by its very nature there was no possibility of discussing it with anyone. Out of this travail came the avalanche of Reality which I attempt to describe.

11

THE EXPERIENCE

WALKING ALONG A CITY STREET one night, feeling inwardly peaceful and content for some unaccountable reason, I glanced into the window of a florist's shop and was startled by the leaf of a plant. This leaf was not different from its neighbors and yet I thrilled in amazement at what I beheld. Something in the motionless leaf was moving. I closed my eyes and then looked again. It was still there—something moved through all the leaves and flowers—it flowed through them like a subtle, vaporous stream, swiftly but without haste. I glanced around to find whether others saw it too, but scores of men and women hurrying by looked into the window and passed on as though it held no mystery.

I watched and marveled for a long time. Intuitively I knew that the vapory, cloudy substance was some kind of life force and presently I wondered why I had never noticed it before, for I also realized that it flows through all leaves and all flowers, everywhere. Except for the first quick shock of surprise it did not appear unnatural. The hardest thing to comprehend was why I hadn't noticed it before.

Then I saw another strange thing. The veins of the leaves stood out in glowing, intricately-woven patterns. Not just the larger veins, but all the tiny hair-like veins which ordinarily are indiscernible. They glowed as though lighted by an inner light, somewhat as phosphorous does in the dark. So vivid were these patterns that they remained in my mind as clear-cut mental images for some time after I left the shop. Without taking thought I knew that these living patterns existed before the material bodies of the leaves were formed, and would continue to exist after the material structures vanished.

I felt a strange kinship toward the leaves and flowers, as though deep down there must be some kind of relationship between us. Then quite suddenly and for just an instant I saw *behind* the patterns and beheld intelligence. Perhaps I did not see it objectively, but I did recognize some form of consciousness and I knew that it recognized me. Something smiled, or gave the impression of smiling, and my heart quickened as though suddenly meeting an old acquaintance.

How long I stood there I have no way of knowing nor do I remember leaving, but I recall walking through a radiant night—walking on air for miles, my mind aglow with the luminous mystery. I knew that what I had seen was neither illusion nor hallucination. I had had visions before and knew that they were visions. This was real.

But so skeptical had I become that the impression of its realness did not remain unchallenged. The fact that I was still partially aware of the luminous patterns and that I could still see a smiling consciousness suggested that it was a grand hoax of my own consciousness. The farther I walked the more insistent grew my doubts and at length I retraced my steps. The streets were almost deserted, but there was still a light in the florist's shop.

One quick glance confirmed my doubts. There was nothing unusual about the display; the leaves and flowers were as cold and lifeless as any other phenomenon of nature. I watched them for some time trying to reproduce the illusion by an imaginative process, but without any success.

This, I thought, is what happens to people who get out of bounds; undoubtedly this is the first step of insanity, or maybe the second, or third. The suggestion that I might be losing my reason did not trouble me greatly, for I had little enough regard for all rational processes. Moreover, in spite of my reasonable doubts there remained a conviction that what I had seen was real. Why I had been unable to see beneath the outward form of the leaves on my second visit I could not understand. I walked home, a distance of several miles, turning the thing over and over in my mind, unable to get rid of the conviction of reality and at the same time unable to overcome my doubts.

When I went to bed I could not sleep. In retrospect the reality of the experience made all argument useless. Again I could see the moving stream of life, the luminous patterns, and the smiling consciousness, and I knew these things were not illusions. Vaguely I became aware of a strange new sensation; something within my being had begun to sing. There were no words nor music, yet it certainly impressed me as a song. It was a mystical sort of rhythm, a movement within my body over which I had no control. It felt as though my whole being moved back and forth in a gentle swaying fashion. Still fearful of illusion I got up and sat motionless in a chair but the movement persisted. It was very pleasant, and when I returned to bed my thoughts began to rise and fall to the inner rhythm. I found myself thinking poetry; the most commonplace thoughts formed themselves into unrhymed verse with no volition nor effort on my part.

I did not attempt to seek the cause of this phenomenon. Coupled with the earlier incident of the evening I felt that some unaccountable change was taking place within my being, but the experience itself was so satisfying that all else was excluded from my consciousness. I lay in bed for hours drinking deeply of this wonderful new rhythm, swaying inwardly in perfect accord with the universe, thrilling to the musical rise and fall of my own thoughts.

I must have slept, for I awoke in the morning to a world full of this vivifying rhythm. My thoughts continued to flow in poetic cadences, and during the night another miracle had occurred: My senses had become abnormally acute, and details of the world about me which had previously escaped my notice were now startlingly vivid. I was conscious of many sounds which I had not heard before, and my senses of sight, touch and smell were also super-normal. I perceived colors which I did not know existed, and now all colors were radiant as though a light shone behind them. In addition to this abnormal sensitivity I became aware of an entirely new sense, or faculty, which correlated all sense perceptions into new categories.

I went about the duties of the morning from force of habit, quite conscious of my actions yet at the same time aware of new meanings in regard to these customary actions. The new sense of perspective revealed relationships which I had never suspected. It was as though I looked down on the world from a great height and beheld the phenomena of the world in their inherent relationships. It was this new capacity for seeing fundamental relationships that revealed new meanings. All things about me and all things connected with my life seemed to lose individual importance yet not one thing appeared unnecessary. The morning shower, breakfast, the house I lived in, my work and the countless details connected with these things formed themselves into new categories or patterns. Startling relationships were revealed. Isolated acts and thoughts which by themselves had previously seemed insignificant now appeared as important factors of larger patterns. Other acts, to which I had always attributed some importance, were now seen as necessary but trivial parts. All acts and all things fitted into place like the pieces of a jigsaw puzzle and occasionally I could catch a glimpse of the whole picture, or at least a vast whole into which many objects and events were welded. I realized that everything has its place and purpose in a great cosmic scheme and that the most insignificant act or word is a part of a larger act or a greater word, and that no act nor word has the meaning we now attribute to it. Meanings and purposes are inherent in the larger acts and the greater words but not in the particulars. The cosmic purposes cannot be known to the personal, human mind unless these larger categories are apprehended.

I realized that not a single act of my life was unnecessary and that not one could have been omitted. There was a moment during which my consciousness expanded and I perceived the whole course of my life; I saw that every word, every act, every struggle and decision had had some bearing and influence on this great moment, and that the experience would have been impossible had one iota been left out. More, I saw that not one single thing could have been omitted—that there are no chance happenings or accidents. Thus I knew that all actions are good, even those which appear base and selfish. A feeling of intense joy, like a wave of irrepressible laughter, swept through my being as this illusion of evil vanished. I saw that there is neither good nor evil but only experience, and that all experiences have a single divine purpose, which purpose I was now experiencing.

12

THE NEW FACULTY

OUR CANARY BEGAN TO SING and with the first notes of the song I awoke with a start, for up to that moment I had not been *fully* conscious. It had not seemed to me that I was asleep—it seemed that I had never been so acutely conscious in my life. The mystic rhythm, new senses, living colors, and the intense joy of the morning were so supernormal that it seemed as though my yesterdays had been spent in a coma. Yet I affirm that up to the moment of that song I was asleep and that all men and women are now asleep though they may believe otherwise. To awaken in the world of reality reveals that all other forms of consciousness are dream states in which we move like animated robots, impelled to actions which we do not understand, and which originate in a section of our being of which we are entirely unaware.

Incomprehensible as it must be to those who believe they are awake, I affirm that our present existence is but a dream-state in contrast to the real waking-state of man, for with the first notes of that song I awoke to a world of radiance with an abrupt start. I felt a vast influx and efflux of power as though a dam had given way, allowing the power of the cosmos to sweep through me in a mighty torrent. All boundaries seemed to recede, all limitations of the senses seemed to vanish. Light poured upon me until I seemed to swim in the brilliant, shimmering, living radiance. It filled my body and my mind, bestowing upon me an intimate, mystical knowledge of the cosmos which is wholly beyond description.

I did not hear the bird singing as we usually hear sounds. I felt the song within; I was both the bird and the song; I was no longer a personality; I was the cosmic stuff which flowed through all things. The song had meaning which I understood; it had meaning in the same sense that words have meaning, but, when I attempted to transcribe the song, I found that it could not be reduced to ideas. Unmistakable and understandable as it was, swelling within me, beating in my heart with exultant power, it nevertheless refused to be limited by words. And as sentimental as the term has become there is only one word by which the nature of this mighty song can be indicated, and that is "love."

Love is the one and only power. It is the originator, flowing through all things to accomplish its own ends. Beyond conception in its mightiness, above all morals, superior to human ideas of justice, indivisible and omniscient, it flows through all things, all beings.

I could no longer stay indoors; it seemed that I must get out into the open to make room for my own expansion. I walked out into a living universe, a fluid world in which all forms were transparent and the inner secrets revealed. I saw life moving in the grass—not the blades of grass moving in the breeze—but an essence moving through them in an unending stream. It was the same miraculous thing I had witnessed the night before in the florist's shop, but now I had become the center through which the life essence flowed.

I had become conscious, not of a new phenomenon, but of an old one. I realized that this had been going on for endless ages, that the universe is a vast ocean of life in which the Soul has always had its existence, and from which it cannot escape. Now, by some miraculous change in my organs of perception I was able to see the essence which only yesterday had been invisible. Life *is* the Reality. It needs no purpose. It is above reason, beyond purpose as we understand the term. To *live,* to express this essence spontaneously and more completely, is purpose incarnate.

I beheld Life in all things both animate and inanimate. I saw it flowing through the bushes and trees, through sticks and stones, pouring through the brown earth. The earth breathes. It breathes just as we do; it pulsates, expands and relaxes. Everything breathes—plants, stones, clouds, the walls of a house—all breathe, all are conscious.

Through a marvelous intuitive faculty which had so suddenly become active I saw *into* the trees and bushes and stones and discovered there mysteries which science can never apprehend. In each thing I perceived its origin, its cosmic purpose or the particular part it plays in the great symphony. I did not investigate the nature of things as we are compelled to do with the physical senses. Through contemplation alone, I became one with the object and thus discovered its inner nature, its cosmic history, why it was and what it was in its totality. For the inner nature of all things is consciousness, which can be contacted and examined through the faculty of intuition.

This new faculty revealed the infinitely small as well as the infinitely large. It penetrated the universe of the atom and expanded to include the uttermost stars. All limitations of consciousness were withdrawn and I moved through the universe at will, into the remote past and the future as well as to the sun and stars.

Through this intuitive faculty I perceived the indivisible unity of the cosmos, for all forms are in reality one body having one Life. I knew that *that* Life is eternal, and that the Soul-existence of every individual is without beginning or end. An infinite sea of Life stretched out on every side, serene and timeless. I also realized that Life is pure, undefiled now and every other now; that the human Soul is undefiled by experience regardless of the nature of the personal experiences.

I saw another marvelous thing which is hard to describe and still more difficult to understand: There is no struggle nor competition in nature. Life moves serenely through all forms without regard for the forms. The physical bodies of plants, animals, men, do not have the importance we attach to them. Each is useful and is serving a cosmic purpose, but viewed from the inner side the *Soul* of things is the real, the important quality, and it is indestructible. Birds, beasts, insects, green things do not contend against each other; one Life moves harmoniously through them all. We see the various forms of nature devouring one another and it seems that they have separate existence but it is not so. There is but one Life essence in which all entities are immersed. It is cosmic, inescapable.

Birth and death are but incidents; there is no extinction of Life, for nothing has life of its own; all entities which have existence now have always existed, for in reality there is neither yesterday nor tomorrow. The phenomena we call birth and death affect only the outer body.

On this higher plane of consciousness there is no imperfection or inconsistency. Every person, every act, every event is in its perfectly appointed place. Sin, sickness, evil and fear vanish entirely. Today as I write this I see the evidence of these things all about me, but I know they are not real, for upon that other plane of consciousness they did not exist.

There was on the other hand a vast consciousness of peace and power—an infinite flow of power, the rhythmic power of the cosmos flowing through me as my very breath and blood, flowing through me to all other things. There were no limitations and I knew I could do all things. Every expression of will was a creative edict. At intervals this awareness of cosmic power lifted me in a swelling ecstasy which sometimes bordered on pain. Looking down on the world the greatest works of mankind—the cities and inventions and empires—appeared as the feeble efforts of children who know not what they are building. So great, and so utterly different are man's higher faculties in contrast to present faculties, that I find no way of describing them which will not appear absurd. Mature as we believe ourselves to be we have not yet progressed beyond the cradle. Man's real powers are still undiscovered, for man is a cosmic Being rather than a reasoning individual.

Individuality! No one can know the meaning of this word until he experiences Reality. Consciousness expands until it embraces all things—until it includes the cosmos. Enveloped in this consciousness I realized the inexplicable truth of Being: The Soul is now infinite; its wisdom and power are limitless; it is not becoming whole or perfect, it is now whole and perfect, since the Soul and the cosmos are one.

There is a higher form of consciousness in which this unity is realized, and it is upon this plane that we shall attain maturity, acquiring powers and faculties which are now far beyond our capacity to imagine.

13

The Radiance

I DO NOT REMEMBER when I returned to the house or whether I responded to my customary and habitual mode of life. I recall only isolated moments, yet I do not attribute this to failure of the memory so much as to the complete loss of the time sense. Time assumed new proportions; it existed but did not elapse. It was not the measuring-stick by which we judge the coming and going of events. It had no relationship to motion, for occasionally motion ceased altogether. There were moments when the earth, the sun, and the stars stood still. Nothing moved except the mystic life.

During these "timeless" periods I experienced an exotic peace which is indescribable. One such moment of peace compensated fully for all the mental suffering I had gone through. Just to stand still and breathe, to feel the ebb and flow of cosmic life through my being, was greater than any pleasure I have ever known.

Moreover, there was a sustained sense of freedom which never diminished during the entire experience. It was as though a thousand bonds had been broken, allowing me to rise to a plane far above the one on which I had been living. This freedom permitted me to move while standing still— to explore a far-distant past which still exists, or to move along the pattern of approaching days. The physical ecstasy of such freedom is unimaginable, and the return to ordinary consciousness was like being cast into a stifling prison in which all freedom of movement is denied. I think now that the greatest pain of returning to ordinary existence was the loss of this sublime freedom.

Here, all about us, is the world of the wondrous, radiant with light, free from the limitations of the senses and all the fears invented by the imagination; it is a world in which we become aware of eternal existence and infinite power. It is a world of consciousness so vast that it appears to be universal. One moves through the cosmos at will by a process of contemplation; one becomes the cosmos and contemplates one's Self.

Yet one does not become the *all*. There is always something other which cannot be embraced—a something which is entirely unknown to the reasoning mind, but for which we do have a word. It appeared to me but a few times, a being far off and unapproachable, yet knowable through the intuitive faculty. There is not a single phase of Reality which can actually be described since words are finite instruments whereas Reality is infinite, yet I find this particular phase much more difficult to write about than any other. Many, many times I have attempted to write about the mystic, unknown Being we call God only to find it utterly impossible to say anything which even remotely indicates the truth.

The Jewish scriptures affirm that man cannot see God, but this is only partially true. It is true in so far as man's normal faculties are concerned, but man has cosmic faculties which not only reveal the invisible forces of nature, but which occasionally reveal that from which these forces emanate. There was revealed to me a Being of magnificent radiance, without form in the accepted sense of the word, but nevertheless a radiance which was knowable as Being.

Between this nameless radiance and the core of my own being there was a wordless interchange of forces which filled me with a super-sexual ecstasy. During these moments there was an intoxicating inflow of power, and a compensating outflow of other forces from my own being. These forces which flowed out from my heart I cannot describe at all; they were forces in the same sense that electricity is a force, yet their essential nature can only be described by the words praise and adoration.

Though I perceived the radiance but once or twice, this interchange of forces was more or less continuous. It was a song of joy which welled spontaneously from the heart and was always compensated by the return of living power. This song, wordless and unthought, rose unceasingly from my being, forming a background or musical accompaniment to existence. But it ebbed and flowed, occasionally swelling to a great crescendo, filling my consciousness completely.

I search for words to describe the other, but find none which even indicate the reality. Rhythm, radiance, love, laughter—of all words these seem to carry a portent. Radiant silent laughter! Joyous loving rhythm! A formless radiance and a soundless laughter, but always radiance and laughter.

14

THE REALITY

I LIVED ON THIS PLANE for three days, at times intensely conscious of the world about me, reveling in the mystic meanings it revealed; at other times ascending to such heights of ecstasy and splendor that the world of forms vanished completely. I think I ate and slept about as usual, yet my appreciation and understanding of such common experiences was vastly increased. I knew intimately, through an intuitive faculty which has since become comparatively inactive, the true purpose of all physical processes. The simplest biological function revealed a spiritual meaning which neither science nor philosophy has vaguely surmised. Every organ and function of the body represents a spiritual characteristic of the cosmos which is now and has always been perfect. The eyes, heart, liver, etc., are not the results of natural selection, they are counterparts of spiritual qualities which are eternal and self-existent. Each one represents an attribute of the invisible and eternal side of the cosmos.

Each physical function is a duplication of a natural spiritual action of the cosmos. The eating of food, for example, represents the flowing quality of the life essence. In reality food is a spiritual substance which, through the marvelous alchemy of the body, is changed from a lower form to a higher form of consciousness. This flow of the life essence through ever-changing forms is not, as science believes, a necessity of the physiological nature; it is a necessity of the spiritual nature of the cosmos. I do not mean that it is possible to live without food. But we do not eat for the sake of physical energy; we partake of food in order to provide a higher form of consciousness for the flow of cosmic forces.

During the three days of this experience the partaking of food gave me an increased physical satisfaction because of my quickened senses, but at the same time it became a sacred rite which was even more intensely satisfying. The act itself became a spiritual communion, a fusion of Being, which in some way produced an inward ecstasy.

For some reason this realization of the fusion of Being remained active for a long time following my return to normal consciousness. The taste of food brought a quickening of all the senses, a swift momentary realization of my cosmic nature, and the spontaneous flow of gratitude from my heart. I know that food is more than "meat" for the body. Like the mating-act it is cosmic rather than individual, and the sensuous gratification from either is only symbolic of a higher ecstasy of which we are at present entirely unaware.

I know also that the personal self and the cosmos are one—that what one does the other does. I do not say that the individual struggle toward the realization of unity is dependent upon the cosmos, for such is not the case. But I affirm that man cannot struggle alone. Behind each man and woman is the entire power and wisdom of an infinite cosmos.

As to the reality of the experience, as to its validity in relation to all other experiences before and since, it stands alone as true. All is illusion except this.

I awoke the morning of the fourth day to a world devoid of light and rhythm, and for a time wandered dazedly in the darkness, praying and hoping for a return of the magnificent freedom. It has not returned in its fullness but there are times when I feel its nearness and bask in the mystic ecstasy of cosmic unity. I know that it will come again and yet again until final emancipation has been achieved. I know also that others shall pass through the same hidden doors, discovering the inner reality, achieving the same glorious freedom.

PART THREE

THE MYSTIC APPROACH TO LIFE

15

SPEAKING A NEW LANGUAGE

FOR SEVERAL MONTHS following this experience I lived in an atmosphere of reflected glory, partially conscious of infinite and eternal existence, sensing my presence in the objects about me, aware of the unity and grandeur of the cosmos. All struggle had vanished and I bathed in the mystic realization of my own completeness. The old familiar "time sense" with its fearful pressure had gone, and my days were filled with an indescribable realization of well-being and peace. I wanted nothing and hoped for nothing better than the continued joy of simple existence.

The time came however when I endeavored to tell others of the mystic beauty of the world in which we live, of its hidden wonders, and of the majesty of the human Soul. It seemed a simple matter to point these things out to others but I soon discovered that such is not the case. In the first place there are no words or combination of words which even begin to convey cosmic meanings. In the second place when one affirms that he has seen things which are invisible to ordinary perception a mental barrier is immediately raised. I know what I tried to relate fell on unhearing minds. Intimate friends began to look at me with a trace of suspicion, and whenever I mentioned Reality I could sense the skepticism and unbelief which greeted my words.

A few tried to understand, realizing that the experience which I attempted to describe had been vital enough to change my entire mode of existence. Yet most of those to whom I talked believed that it was nothing more than a religious conversion. Some, I am quite sure, considered it pathological.

No doubt the fault was largely mine for I was unable to talk about it rationally. Aware of the eternal existence I could laugh at the absurdity of birth and death, but if I attempted to express the reality of human existence, about all I could do was to make the meaningless statement that the Soul is eternal, and that I *knew* it was eternal because I had lived in eternity for three days.

If I attempted to point out the unreality of good and evil, of sickness and health, or the apparent duality of will, I at once took a position contrary to human experience. I was, in fact, actually affirming that the world as all the rest of humanity sees it, is an illusion!

For some time I did not realize the incongruity of the situation. Even the story of the fond mother, which was told by a close and well-meaning friend, made no impression upon me: A mother, watching a parade in which her son was taking part, proudly exclaimed, "They are all out of step but my Johnny." I could not alter my position however absurd it might appear to others, for I still lived on the borderland of a realm of consciousness where the inner reality of all things is perceived.

From personal experience I knew the world of three dimensions as well as anyone, but I had also been inducted into a realm of consciousness where Reality is known first-hand through faculties which are superior to our intellectual faculties. Thus I had seen the world from two standpoints and I knew there was no correspondence whatever between the rational world of the mind and the world of cosmic Reality.

Of one thing I became increasingly certain: This world of infinite splendor into which I had been mysteriously inducted was the very thing which Jesus proclaimed and which he called the Kingdom of Heaven. And this experience was identical in its fundamental nature with the illuminating experiences of Saint Paul, St. John, Mohammed, Ramakrishna, Kabir and others. For in the teaching of all the great spiritual leaders I now found a common theme—one which the world in general has never understood because it is so unequivocally counter-rational. Without exception, they affirm that the world as we know it is an illusion.

Mankind, they affirm, is marching solidly together, but getting exactly nowhere. Our movement is not even forward, for we run upon an endless belt, a treadmill, the motion of which leads us to believe that we are getting somewhere. We have reached a level of consciousness which in itself is good, for it is part of the great cosmic scheme. But the world of duality, or reason, is but one of many worlds in the universal pattern, and the progress of the human Soul cannot be measured by a translational movement. Progress is determined by our movement away from the world of reason.

We of the mechanical age are quite certain that we are making progress. By comparing our present mechanized status with the old horse-and-buggy days we conclude that we are indeed making great forward strides, and we feel justly proud when some of our scientific spokesmen tell us that we have made more progress during the past fifty or one-hundred years than mankind made in any previous thousand year period. We have witnessed many changes, but it does not follow that these changes constitute progress. If progress means the swift deterioration of the body, increased nervous tension and enormously increased fear complex, vast numbers of unemployed, the most devastating wars the world has ever known, endless-belt production which is turning human beings into unthinking cogs, huge parasitic labor organizations which enslave rather than emancipate working men, and a vast complicated system of civil and criminal laws which is now beyond the human capacity to administer, but to which we add new laws in ever-increasing numbers, then we are indeed making progress.

If we take a longer view and compare the present civilization with some which have long since passed into oblivion we may get a better idea of the treadmill. For aside from our mechanical inventions we are less advanced than many of our predecessors, notably those civilizations which constructed our present systems of logic, arithmetic, algebra, geometry, engineering and civil laws, and which discovered and formulated the principles of music, literature, art, sculpturing and the classic dance. Accepting these things ready-made as a heritage from other civilizations we have been unable to approach the heights of culture which they reached.

Taking a still longer view we find there is less to be proud of, for in regard to the real problems of life and the great questions of the Soul there has been no progress whatever. There is within us the same insistent demand to know who we are, why we are here, and where we are going, that troubled the first civilized men and women. Toward the solving of these really important questions we have not taken one progressive step, for with all our scientific knowledge we are as ignorant concerning these matters as the people of a civilization which may have existed, according to some archaeologists, not ten thousand years ago, but more than a million years ago.

Are these questions insoluble? Do we live in a universe which we can never really *know?* Is there no way by which we can escape the treadmill?

There has always been a way of emancipation: it is the way announced by all the messiahs of the race, and it is essentially a movement in a new direction. A new direction cannot *parallel* the treadmill, i.e., it cannot be similar to our present form of consciousness but on a slightly higher level. It must be toward a different realm, one which has been named the Fourth Dimension by such thinkers as C.H. Hinton and P.D. Ouspensky—the same realm which Jesus called the Kingdom of Heaven, which Gautama called Nirvana, which Chuang Tze called Tao, and which Edward Carpenter and Dr. Maurice Bucke called Cosmic Consciousness.

In the years which have elapsed since my induction into the world of infinities I have found many other initiates, some of whom are known throughout the civilized world. These men and women have all left a memorial, or testimony, regarding their initiation into and knowledge of the world of reality. Dr. Bucke has assembled a great deal of this testimony in his book *Cosmic Consciousness,* and has given us the key which distinguishes this testimony from all other writings.

In Shakespeare's *Tempest* and in some of the sonnets the secret of his great vision is revealed; in Plato's *Republic,* in Balzac's *Seraphita,* in Dante's *Vita Nuova,* there is unmistakable evidence of cosmic vision. In the writings of William Blake, Edward Carpenter, Jacob Boehme, in the poems of Browning, Tennyson, Goethe, the Songs of Solomon, and especially in the magnificent poems of Walt Whitman there is direct evidence of cosmic initiation. In the works of Blavatsky, Mable Collins, Plotinus, Hinton, Claude Bragdon, Paul Brunton, Dr. Van der Leeuw and Evelyn Underhill, Cosmic Consciousness is the common theme.

These are but a few of the men and women of a growing company which speaks a new language—the language of the Soul which is so evident in the works of Socrates, Richard Wagner, Raphael, Tagore, Swedenborg, Justinian, Saint Teresa and Annie Besant.

The discovery of this growing company was indeed inspiring. I no longer felt quite so alone, for I confess quite frankly that my position has never changed regardless of its apparent absurdity. In the pursuit of intellectual knowledge mankind is not going anywhere. The belief that progress is inevitable and that it results from the scientific investigation of a three-dimensional world is, in the largest sense, erroneous.

Humanity is imprisoned within a field of consciousness which produces one civilization after another. Each lives for a while, makes some minor contribution, grows old and dies. And all but a comparatively few men and women of these civilizations live and die without discovering who they are, what the struggle is all about, whence they came and whither bound. A few escape the treadmill by making a seemingly perilous leap in the dark—by simply stepping off the endless belt and striking out on a new perpendicular.

More than a decade of study has led me to believe that most if not all of the men and women who have achieved Cosmic Consciousness have found their way through the darkness without any foreknowledge of what awaited them, and without realizing the absolute and unvarying requisites for initiation. Like myself they felt a growing desire for first-hand knowledge of Reality and simply refused to be satisfied with less. This conclusion has been forced upon me by the lack of comment on this particular phase of the subject.

Some investigators like Dr. Bucke and William James who made a study of the psychological aspects of Cosmic Consciousness failed to discover the key to its attainment. Others like Hinton and Ouspensky believe that an entirely new mental culture is necessary. Many of the modem adepts like Edward Carpenter and Paul Brunton find the solution in the practices of the Indian Yoga, or in adaptations of these ancient practices. Some of the great initiates like Blake, Whitman, Goethe, scarcely mention the secret of their attainment.

The "secret" is no secret at all. It has been proclaimed by every great religious teacher of the race. But largely because we have looked upon these teachings as "religious" in the narrowest sense of the word, believing that they represent moral or ethical codes only, we have failed to grasp the stupendous significance of the changeless doctrine. In essence it is this: There is another and vastly superior side to our being; this fourth side is the important one since it is causal, containing the mysterious realizations of eternal life and infinite wisdom. It is the realm of "lightning-like splendors," of magnificent freedoms and the "peace which passeth human understanding"; and it is the only one through which we can "know the Eternal, who he is and what his works are." The ever-reiterated "secret" of attainment is simply stated: The complete and unequivocal rejection of the world, or the form of consciousness which now enslaves us.

The "far-off divine event" toward which mankind is moving—or toward which we as individuals can move—is a higher form of 'self-awareness.' It is not a state of mind which can be cultivated by rational methods, but a state of consciousness which must be achieved by a transition.

16

UNDERSTANDING CONSCIOUSNESS

I BELIEVE IT IS IMPOSSIBLE for most of us to attempt this transition without a partial understanding of the nature of consciousness. Now, as always, a few will be able to do so, but generally speaking we have become so ultra-rational that emancipation is very difficult. It appears to us that our present form of consciousness is "final"; that it is the natural estate; that our scientific knowledge of the world is the essence of reality. Thus we do not even consider the possibility of a higher form of human consciousness which might be our true estate, and where knowledge is replaced by intuitive wisdom.

With the help of others I have been able to reconstruct the ancient doctrine of the "four worlds" of consciousness which I submit in the briefest possible form, hoping it may be of value to the truth-seekers of a scientific era. Reference to these several worlds is made time and again in Oriental scriptures, but it is in the works of Kant, James, Bucke, and Ouspensky that we find the key to understanding.

In the *Critique of Pure Reason,* Immanuel Kant establishes one of the basic premises upon which most of the ancient wisdom schools were founded; namely, that the world in which we live, move, and have our being, is one of consciousness. This world of consciousness we can and do know to its conceptual limits, but there is a "ring-pass-not" which encircles us making it impossible for us to know what the real world might be like in its essential nature.

In a measure I have already shown why this must be so. The real world is infinite, our knowledge about it is fragmentary, finite. This being so, we do not "see" the world at all; what we actually perceive is a mental image of the world—a complicated world-image made up of smaller images of people, events, ideas and conditions.

In reality these individual world-images consist of our thoughts and feelings about things, while the things-in-themselves are unknown. In other words we do not contact the world directly. We think that we do, for traditionally we think in terms of the physical instrument, or body. Thus when we take an orange in our hands we say that we are contacting one of the objects of the external world directly. But the 'knower' is within and is aware only of the sensations which the orange produces in consciousness. These sensations, or percepts, are formed into mental images to which we give names, but neither the images nor the names correspond with the reality. Through the same limited sense-channels we can discover the chemical constituency of an orange and other peculiarities of its make-up, but no matter how far we extend our investigations we never discover what it is that produces the sensations.

Science affirms that in its ultimate nature an orange is energy, but this statement is not one whit more enlightening than the former scientific assertion that it was matter. Either one, energy or matter, can be known to us only as an idea. Matter itself is a concept. Once the concept "matter" has been formed in our minds we can think matter, and we can think many other thoughts about matter, but the thing itself is unknowable.

Contrary to popular belief the mind does not "photograph" the objects which surround us. It makes mechanical sensations of sight, touch, smell, taste and sound, and from them constructs new forms. These composite forms are called recepts, but they are not the units with which we think. A recept is a cumbersome, unwieldy thing; it may consist of hundreds or thousands of percepts drawn from countless contacts with a particular kind of object. These recepts are stored in the subjective levels of consciousness and we no longer deal with them directly. We have tagged them, given them names, and in the foreground of consciousness where we think, we deal only with the names.

Why does memory not take us back to the moment of birth, or at least to the early days of childhood? It is because concepts (or named recepts) did not exist for us. During the first months of our existence we lived in a world of chaos—a world of instinct, emotion, and unorganized sense perceptions. As the number of percepts increased the mind correlated them into orderly groups. Our emotions, personal tendencies and natural instincts made their contributions to these clusters of sensations, and the blurred objects about us began to acquire form.

Not in the outer world did these new forms appear, but in the same place that new forms now appear—in consciousness. In other words we began to create new worlds—entirely personal world-images which have no counterpart in nature. And the knowable forms of these world-images are the recepts to which we have given names.

The creative process by which new worlds are formed has never stopped, but it is not in the stellar reaches that we need look for evidence. The process takes place in our minds. Out of the primordial substance of consciousness comes the creation of new forms over which we henceforth exercise dominion.

Each of us is the original Adam and infancy is the Garden of Eden. Infancy represents a form of consciousness where likenesses and differences are not perceived; there is neither good nor evil, pride nor shame. Opposites are unknown. Only the most primitive forms (recepts or subjective images) exist and these forms are nameless. Like the other Adam we are confronted with the enormous task of naming all the plants, animals, toys and people, for each receptual image must have its special tag.

Furthermore, it is through woman or the tireless care and patience of the mother that we are enticed out of the garden of non-discrimination into a state of self-consciousness. Over and over the mother seeks to impress the meaning of words upon the infant mind, and is overjoyed when the "light of reason" begins to dawn. For this light is evidenced by the use of words—words which represent the intricate "clusters of sensations" which constitute our inner worlds of consciousness.

Like the other Adam we soon find ourselves in an alien world. We are soon ashamed of our nakedness for our vision is now dual; we perceive both nakedness and non-nakedness and reason that one is good, and the other evil. We are now self-conscious beings, dividing being into self and not-self, pain and pleasure, sickness and health, and an endless array of opposites. Here we dream and aspire but never find complete satisfaction. We long for a better world, confused by our own knowledge and the theories which are nothing but words, tormented by the subjective memory of our lost estate.

This is the esoteric meaning of the familiar story, and it means that we live in worlds of our own making, knowing all things inwardly by virtue of the images produced in consciousness. These images are tagged and by their names we know and use them. The real world is foreign, unknown in its true nature. It does not correspond, is not a replica, is not identical with our conceptions. Images and names, emotions and instincts—these are the things of which our inner worlds consist—and whatever meaning life appears to have we have given it by use of the imagination.

In the mystical story of the creation there is one implication which must not be overlooked, for it represents the basic tenet of the 'great doctrine.' The tree which was responsible for Adam's (or humanity's) entrance into a higher form of consciousness was the "tree of the knowledge of good and evil." The fruit of this symbolical tree made the conception of opposites possible. In other words, it lifted mankind from the stygian darkness of emotionalism to rational self-consciousness. But the story does not end here; there is yet another tree, the fruit of which will lift man from the comparative darkness of rationalism to a radiant world of infinities.

To reach this other tree—the tree of life—we must face the terrors of a "flaming sword." Rather, we must face the mental darkness which this invisible sword produces. For this is the same sword which Jesus talked about, the sword which destroys our rational beliefs, setting us adrift on an unknown sea of consciousness.

The implication that there is another and higher form of consciousness which enables us to realize eternal life and the infinity of being is unmistakable. It is this implication which philosophy and theology have so consistently ignored or misinterpreted, and which a science-minded humanity must recognize if there is to be further progress.

It is this spiritual curiosity or unquenchable desire to know, coupled with the realization that we cannot know by means of the intellect, that increases our sensitivity to higher faculties of the Soul through which we can know.

This kind of mysticism does not demand seclusion, or at least it does not demand our permanent withdrawal from society. We will find periods of solitude increasingly valuable, for there will be times when perspective is enlarged by an aloofness from the noise and confusion of ordinary existence. But it is my earnest conviction that we of the West must wage the battle for emancipation in the midst of activity. This coincides with Plato's viewpoint, for in the Orient where he traveled after his own initiation he found the most enlightened men living in the midst of, but aloof from, the most decadent civilization.

If our civilization continues, and it is possible that ours is the one through which a major transition can be made, its existence will depend on two things, both of which are fairly obvious. There must be a transition to a higher form of consciousness on a large scale, and the men and women who achieve Cosmic Consciousness must remain active in human affairs. Thus they will act as the "leavening agents" which will "leaven the whole lump."

There is evidence which indicates that this is the appointed time. Never before in the long history of the race has there been such a wide-spread demand for freedom, nor has there been such a realization of the unity of the peoples of the earth. Never has there been such a demand for a new and better way of life, coupled with a growing distrust in the ability of our political and industrial leaders to show us the way. And perhaps never in the history of Christianity has there been so much skepticism regarding traditional, organized religion and its methods.

17

APPROACHING SOUL REALIZATION

In *THE VARIETIES OF RELIGIOUS EXPERIENCE*, William James records the following conclusions: "The whole drift of my education goes to persuade me that the world of our present consciousness is but one out of many worlds of consciousness that exist.... . The further limits of our being, plunge, it seems to me, into an altogether other dimension of existence from the sensible and merely 'understandable' world. Name it the mystical region, or the supernatural region ... we belong to it in a more intimate sense than that in which we belong to the visible world."

These are indeed arresting conclusions, especially so when they come from a highly honored member of a scientific fraternity which often ridicules the super-natural. Yet they are conclusions which psychology and philosophy should have deduced long ago. Mankind has already progressed through two distinct stages of mental development and is now progressing through a third. These three stages are so different from each other, involving such diverse powers, behavior, and results, that they cannot be considered as a single type of consciousness.

During the first long period of racial development man's consciousness was very elemental. Knowledge consisted of nothing more than the perception of sense stimuli which induced instinctive responses. That man once existed in such a primitive state is common knowledge; the point is that this very primitiveness was due to an elemental type of consciousness which did not reveal form, color, meanings, or even the fact of self-existence. Man's entire "world" consisted of unrelated and meaningless percepts.

The second stage was reached when through constant repetition and overlapping of percepts certain recepts were formed. The birth of receptual intelligence marked man's entrance into a higher form of consciousness and endowed him with new powers. Whereas before he was aware of sense impressions only and knew not whence they came or even that an objective world existed, he was now able to perceive the forms of the objects which pleased or irritated him. He was thus enabled to react emotionally as well as instinctively to his environment. In short, he progressed from an instinctive to an emotional state.

The third stage was reached when man was able to substitute a word for a recept. We know this transition was not achieved overnight, that the human race did not awaken one morning to find itself in the possession of language. It was a slow, gradual movement, but there came a time when some man or woman uttered the first word. It was a single, spontaneous utterance of the word which has ever since been on man's lips; that first word was "I," for by this transition man reached the plane of self-consciousness. He recognized himself as an entity, as something apart from his environment.

With this new birth came the most amazing revelations. For the first time man realized that the life which seemed to motivate trees and other objects of his hazy environment was in himself. The tree which only yesterday had threatened him, the boulders which appeared to rush upon him, the cave which seemed to approach with open jaws, were now motionless. He moved, but they remained stationary.

In a single stroke the power of many of his old enemies was destroyed by this realization of self-hood. He looked down on his companions as from a great height and knew they were asleep, that they moved aimlessly about in his former prison. He perceived unities which were incomprehensible to his fellows, for now trees, stones, caves were related by a common earth.

It is not likely that the realization of self-hood was continuous. The transition must have required several initiatory experiences, and the real significance of these initiations could not have been fully comprehended. Undoubtedly they increased in intensity and scope until a continuous realization of self as opposed to the world was achieved.

How long the word "I" sufficed cannot be estimated, but from this fundamental realization of a "cupful of reality" man has not yet progressed. Today the reality is still unknown. All that we know, or have taken time to know, are the thoughts which parade across the foreground of consciousness.

These stages of man's development are not foreign to our experience. The cycles are re-lived in the recapitulatory process which begins with fetal conception. Thus in a single lifetime we have experienced three distinctly different forms of consciousness, each having certain limitations, and each endowing us with a specific power. These forms of consciousness may be summarized as follows:

(1) Simple-consciousness which is similar to if not identical with the type of consciousness common to plants and the lower forms of animal life. This is the kind of consciousness we had during the embryonic period. It is essentially physical and its one form of knowledge consisted of percepts, its one form of power was instinct.

(2) Emotional-consciousness which is similar to the form now evidenced by the higher types of animals. It is the state into which we were "born," and the plane upon which we lived for about two years. Here our knowledge of the world was enlarged into recepts, and the second great power we acquired was emotion.

(3) Self-consciousness, a form not shared by any other type of being on this planet. Here the knowledge of the world was broadened to three dimensions; we acquired three-dimensional mental images or concepts, and the third great power is reason.

Each of these forms of consciousness corresponds to a different phase of man's being: The first to his physical nature, the second to his emotional nature, and the third to his mental nature. But this does not complete the "square" of being, for man has a spiritual nature and his spiritual aspirations are just as real as his physical needs, his loves and hates, his mental schemes and intellectual hopes. We are forced to conclude that there must be a form of consciousness which corresponds to the spiritual nature and thus we must add one more form to the above categories:

(4) Cosmic-Consciousness which is Soul-realization. Here the knowledge of the world is broadened by the recognition of still another dimension of space, which is the world of cause. And the fourth great power which man acquires by this transition is intuition, a faculty which contacts and perceives the infinite world directly.

18

PERCEIVING THE FOURTH DIMENSION

IT IS NOT LIKELY that the four categories which we have listed are fictitious. Many of our ideas about them may be, but that there are four sides to man's being is unquestionable. Body, emotion, mind, spirit, represent real divisions of some sort. Knowledge has always divided itself into these categories; the divisions exist because of some underlying and changeless reality.

Materialistic science would like to eliminate one of these categories simply because scientific methods do not permit an exploration of this field, but the efforts of science to eliminate the spiritual realm succeed only in making the world more and more difficult for the scientist to understand.

A few leaders like Oumoff, Minkowsky and Einstein have questioned the validity of the human conception of space but science as a whole has evinced little interest in the matter. As long ago as 1911, Professor Oumoff demonstrated that our present idea of space does not correspond with cosmic space. There is, he affirmed, another dimension of space which we are unable to perceive in its entirety, but which reveals itself to us in small segments. This fourth dimension of space we now call time. As an extension of space it exists but does not transpire. We apprehend this invisible dimension little by little and interpret our own mental effort as an external motion, or a progression of things in time. This illusion, he declared, gives us a faulty impression of the universe; what the real four-dimensional world might be like, we do not know.

It was this latter conclusion no doubt which consigned Oumoff's findings to oblivion. Our scientific knowledge of the world is so enormous and has been gathered with such meticulous care that we are loathe to part with it. We are willing to admit that the evidence of our senses is sometimes misleading, and that many of our early scientific theories were erroneous, but we simply cannot admit that all of our knowledge of the world is illusory. Nevertheless, this is just what we are compelled to do if there is another dimension of space.

Ouspensky has shown us why this is so in *Tertium Organum*. A being with two-dimensional consciousness would recognize but two extensions of space, length and width. Our third dimension, depth, would be partially apprehended, but not as an extension of space; it would be cognized as time, or as a strange phenomenon which somehow caused a movement of objects in its world. In traveling around a house, for instance, it would appear to such a being that one side disappeared into the "past" while another side appeared out of the "future," for the being is not aware of its own movement. Only by achieving Self-consciousness could the being distinguish between its own motion and the illusory motion of objects in its environment.

Our predicament is analogous. Unable to cognize the fourth dimension of space we are deceived by appearances and translate our own mental efforts as a movement of things in time. Four-dimensional structures exist; they do not appear out of a mythical future and disappear into a mythical past. It is our deficiency of vision which produces the illusion of a changing world.

We know that a being unable to perceive depth, unable to understand the phenomenon of angles, and therefore unable to realize the manner in which plane surfaces are unified as solids, would also be unable to arrive at a single correct conclusion regarding the three-dimensional world. And could such beings reason it is obvious that none of their conclusions regarding the phenomena of nature, the movement of bodies, cause and effect, universal laws, would be correct. Some would not be true and others false; in regard to the nature of a three-dimensional world, all the conclusions of a two-dimensional being would be false.

For the same cause—limitations of consciousness—none of our conclusions regarding the nature of an infinite universe can be true. The scientific hypotheses constructed from a growing mass of three-dimensional evidence do not represent the cosmos or the manner in which it operates. We know, of course, that they are not final; we must realize that they are not true.

To what, then, does our knowledge apply? To an imaginary world which has no real existence, or which exists only by virtue of incomplete and therefore incorrect receptual images to which we have given names. This is the three-dimensional world of reason which we must reject if there is to be further progress.

19

EXPERIENCING THE SIXTH SENSE

IF WE NOW PROCEED in the opposite direction, increasing instead of decreasing the sensuous apprehension of the world, several things become clear. The form of consciousness would change revealing a vaster, more complex, and at the same time a more unified world. We would suddenly find ourselves in a universe from which most of the motion of objects had disappeared, and the larger objects would disclose new meanings and purposes.

Self would also be realized differently. In this case we must say that awareness of self as a person gives way to an awareness of Self as the cosmos. "I am" is replaced by the realization, "I am 'that'; all that is, was, or ever will be; the totality of things, eternal, infinite, perfect, complete."

As each form of human consciousness has endowed us with a specific form of power—first instinct, then emotion, and finally reason—we may expect the addition of a new and superior form of power. As previously noted this new power is intuition and it permits us to contact the inner side of things, to know cause.

This new power is far more than a psychic faculty which occasionally prompts us or indicates the right direction, though it certainly does this if we continue in the search for Reality. Intuition is a combination of Soul-faculties, analogous to our present mental faculties. But, whereas our mental faculties try to make a whole cloth out of the

113

variegated threads of experience, the Soul-faculties lift us above such finite efforts to a contemplation of the infinite.

St. Paul tried to convey some idea of the marvelous power of intuition in his letter to the Corinthians. "For now we know in part, and we prophecy (or make conclusions) in part. But when that which is perfect is come, then that which is in part will be done away. (The rational faculties will assume a subordinate role, just as instinct and emotion have done). When I was a child (a rational being) I spake as a child, I understood as a child, I thought as a child; but when I became a man {a four-square being) I put away childish things. For now we see through a glass darkly; but then face to face; now I know in part; but then I shall know even as I am known."

Edward Carpenter has given us a more understandable description in his book, *From Adam's Peak to Elephanta:* "The individual consciousness takes the form of thought, which is fluid and mobile like quicksilver, perpetually in a state of change and unrest, fraught with pain and effort; the other consciousness is not in the form of thought. It touches, sees, bears, and *is* those things which it perceives—without motion, without effort, without change, without distinction of subject and object, but with a vast and incredible joy."

Dr. Bucke throws a little more light on the subject, showing how increased sensitivity produces a realization of "livingness." "This consciousness shows the cosmos to consist not of dead matter governed by unconscious, rigid and unintending laws; it shows it on the contrary as entirely immaterial, entirely spiritual, and entirely alive; it shows that death is an absurdity, that everyone and everything has eternal life.

"He does not come to believe merely, but he sees and knows that the cosmos, which to the self-conscious mind seems to be made up of dead matter, is in fact far otherwise—it is in truth a 'living presence'. He sees that instead of men being, as it were, patches of life scattered through an infinite sea of non-living substance, they are in reality specks of relative death in an infinite ocean of life. He sees that the life which is in man is eternal, as all life is eternal, and that the Soul of man is as immortal as God is.

"A man learns infinitely much of the new. Especially does he obtain such a conception of the whole—or at least of an immense whole—as dwarfs all conception, imagination or speculation, such a conception as makes the old attempts to mentally grasp the universe and its meanings petty and even ridiculous."

Ouspensky is even more direct. Regarding the nature of the universe as it is disclosed by the intuitive mind, he says: "There is nothing dead or unconscious. Everything lives, everything breathes, thinks, feels; everything is conscious and everything speaks."

This, in essence, is the testimony of most of the men and women who have succeeded in bridging the gap which separates the world of reason from the world of intuitional consciousness. It is this same magnificent form of consciousness which the early Christian mystics called the "Christ Mind," and which Jesus himself called the "Kingdom of Heaven."

Since time immemorial the existence of a sixth sense has been known, and it has been designated by various names, "the single eye," which does not cognize opposites; the "all-seeing eye" which comprehends infinity; the "eye of the Soul" which perceives the invisible; the "spiritual eye" by which the unnamed cause is apprehended.

It is by and through this sixth sense, or the intuitive faculty, that we are inducted into an infinite universe and are appraised of our own eternalness. We become the cosmos, and not theoretically or by an imaginative process, but through an expansion of consciousness.

Plotinus tells the same thing in his *Letter to Flaccus:* "You ask, how can we know the Infinite? I answer, not by reason. It is the office of reason to distinguish and define. The Infinite cannot therefore be ranked among its objects. You can only apprehend the Infinite by a faculty which is superior to reason, by entering into a state where you are your finite self no longer—in which the divine essence is communicated to you. This is ecstasy. It is the liberation of your mind from its finite consciousness. Like can only apprehend like; when you thus cease to be finite you become one with the Infinite... . But this sublime condition is not of permanent duration. It is only now and then that we can enjoy this elevation above the limits of the body and the world. I, myself, have realized it but three times as yet, and Porphyry hitherto not once."

Jacob Boehme tried to describe the nature of intuitive perception in the account of his third induction. "The gate was opened to me," he says quite simply, "and in one quarter of an hour I saw and knew more than if I had been many years at a university... . I knew and saw myself in all three worlds ... and likewise how the fruitful bearing womb of eternity (the fourth world) brought forth. So that I did not only greatly wonder at it but did exceedingly rejoice.

"Suddenly my spirit did break through ... even unto the innermost birth of Geniture and Deity, and there I was embraced with love, as a bridegroom embraces his dearly beloved bride. But the greatness of this triumphing that was in the spirit I cannot express either in speaking or writing; neither can it be compared to anything but that wherein life is generated in the midst of death, and it is like the resurrection of the dead.

"In this light my spirit suddenly saw through all, and in and by all creatures; even in the herbs and grass it knew God, who he is, and how he is, and what his work is."

From these accounts we may be quite sure that initiation into the realm of infinity does not endow one with omniscience. One discovers the nature of the 'great scheme,' the unity of all things and the "eternalness" of life, but the contemplation of the mystery of an infinite magnitude requires eternity—there is no end to it. And profound, ecstatic, and limitless as one's realizations are the return to normal consciousness is inevitable. These experiences are initiatory only, similar to the fragmentary realizations of self-hood which once prepared man for entrance into the world of three dimensions.

The full significance of Soul-consciousness cannot be known, even by those who occasionally pass through its portals. Just as primitive man could not have known the portent of self-awareness nor have foreseen the potentialities of conceptual intelligence with its accompanying civilizations, neither can we begin to estimate the full portent of Cosmic Consciousness.

It is apparent that the square of being is not complete, and that our present form of consciousness cannot be man's true estate. There are powers and capacities as yet unknown and untapped, faculties which reveal a world "as dwarfs all conception, imagination and speculation." It is here, in the realm of Cosmic Consciousness, that we discover the Soul and its mystic powers; and it is here that we may expect to reach perfection, becoming what Wells so aptly termed "God-like Men."

20

LIVING UNDER GRACE

WITH EVEN A PARTIAL understanding of the nature of consciousness it becomes obvious that human progress cannot long be measured by intellectual development. As necessary and important as it is in its place—and of this there is no question—the intellect cannot lead us out of the conflict of opposites. War and peace, sickness and health, love and hate, famine and plenty, are inherent in our present form of consciousness. We cannot reason our way into Utopia, for by its very nature reason produces opposing opinions and is thus the creator of conflict.

More than twenty-five centuries ago Plato pointed out that war and science are twins, and that the more scientific nations become, the more certain and devastating will be their commercial and military conflicts. The most superficial study of the rise and fall of civilizations confirms Plato's observation, yet we have become so thoroughly inoculated with the "germ of science" that we see but one side of the picture. We believe that knowledge—more and more scientific knowledge—will solve our problems. We hold to this position even when we see that every apparent advance creates not one but two additional problems, and the solving of these gives rise to four, and these to sixteen, and so on endlessly.

The truth is we are no longer making progress. We are fighting windmills with broken spears, treading methodically up and down on an illusory hypothesis of existence. Like Don Quixote we have become so enamored of our imaginary ideals that we fail to see the illusoriness of our little world. Above the clamor and confusion can be heard the strident voices of scientists, educators, politicians, crying that all is well, and that we are now on our way to a beautiful utopia. But the voices—persuasive, reasonable, superior—are similar to those which barked for the side-shows of life in other civilizations. Calling attention to the marvels of science, to the great strides being made in the fields of education and government, mankind is hypnotized into believing that rational existence is indeed the big show, and that all we need is more of the same thing.

The developments of modem science are indeed phenomenal, and as I have pointed out there is no need for us to reject the fruits of science in order to achieve a higher form of consciousness. But we must free ourselves from the belief that scientific knowledge represents truth, and that further progress is possible by a continued translational movement. This apparent progress is not only illusory, but it is the very will-'o-the-wisp that leads to destruction of civilizations.

If we detach ourselves from the present moment we see that we are no more capable of constructing a true hypothesis of cosmogony than our predecessors. Certainly we have more factual knowledge on which to base our hypothesis than had the philosophers and scientists of other days, but the factual knowledge is of the same kind. It is three-dimensional knowledge of a universe which is not three-dimensional.

All of our facts are conditioned by a three-dimensional conception of space, by a realization of time which does not correspond with cosmic time, and a mental astigmatism which does not permit us to distinguish self-motion from true motion. Our scientific hypotheses regarding the nature of the world appear to be true since we are all bound by the same limitations. That is, it seems to us that science cannot be wrong regarding the shape of the earth, its axial and cyclic movements, etc. Nevertheless, we must remember that these are conclusions produced by a faulty instrument from incomplete sense evidence. They do not represent the thing itself. They merely tell us how the world appears to look and act when viewed through the very narrow aperture of rational consciousness. The earth, time, motion, will of necessity have to be different if there is another dimension of space. What a four-dimensional world might look like, how the objects of the three-dimensional world might be unified, what true motion and cosmic time might be like, science does not know, nor can it know through its methods of investigation.

The theory that we can reconstruct the universal plan by means of analogy—through the doctrine of microcosm and macrocosm—is thus pure fallacy. We construct nothing but a huge, three-dimensional world-image which cannot correspond with an infinite cosmos. The great axiom of Hermes, "As above, so below," does not permit a literal interpretation. It does indicate the oneness of principle, but it does not follow that our "reading of the mirrors" is correct.

As an example, the action we see in nature and which we interpret as universal law cannot correspond with the force-itself. Our "law of gravitation" is simply a statement of the manner in which *we* observe the action of an unknown cosmic force. What that force might be or how it manifests universally we do not know. Beings with fewer than five senses will observe the action differently and the knowledge derived from the observations will be different from ours. Likewise a being with more than five senses will perceive the action differently and thus have a different knowledge of the law. To the latter the cosmic force will appear in its infinite relationships, which means that it will appear both constant and variable, containing the possibility of action and non-action. This violates our concept of law, for in order to be classified as law a force must be constant, non-variable.

Our so-called natural laws express our own limitations but they tell us nothing about the real nature of cosmic forces. Every person knows that eyes are necessary for seeing and that ears are needed for hearing; but every initiate knows that it is possible to see without eyes and hear without ears. Everyone knows that we cannot be in two places at the same time, yet this is not a universal law; distance and time are not obstacles for the initiate since he can be in many places at the same moment. We all know that the essence we call life is invisible and that the most powerful microscope is unable to detect it; yet it is plainly visible through the sixth sense. Every physicist knows that two objects cannot occupy the same space at the same time; yet the initiate knows that many objects occupy the same four-dimensional space at all times. The phenomena of birth and death are unquestionable scientific facts and they certainly appear as opposing facts; but to the initiate they appear as the same phenomenon.

Every "natural law" of our rational world is contradicted by experience in the realm of the Soul. The very concept "law" is contradicted, for in the realm of the Soul there are no limitations—all things are infinite and therefore not bound in any way.

The cosmos is not what it seems to be; it is not what we are trying to make it by our reason. It is far more wonderful, fluid, and spontaneous than we have imagined. To us it appears dead, governed by laws which are unintelligent and limited. It is our own form of consciousness which is unintelligent and limited. Actually we have our being in a universe of radiant splendor, eternal mystery, pulsating life; it is we who are dead, not the cosmos. We are sleepers, dreaming we are awake. And the "world" which seems so real to us has no more substance than the fantastic worlds of our lesser dreams and nightmares.

The concept of a universal creation as a movement which is proceeding-in-time is an illusion, one of our dreams. Could we suddenly open our "inner eye" we would see all things in their entirety and the illusion of external motion would vanish. We would see that all things are infinite, without beginning or ending. About them we could say that they *are*, and that what they are now they have always been and always will be, eternal and changeless. We would realize being, and know that the sense of *becoming* was an illusion, produced by a form of consciousness which does not permit the perception of truth. Thus would we understand that all human knowledge is erroneous; that all "natural laws" are statements regarding a form of consciousness and are not applicable to other forms nor to the cosmos itself.

In one of his meditations Chuang Tze summarizes the predicament in which humanity finds itself. He says: "You cannot speak of ocean to a well-frog, the creature of a narrower sphere. You cannot speak of ice to a summer insect, the creature of a season. You cannot speak of Tao to a pedagogue, his scope is too restricted. But now you have emerged from your narrow sphere and have glimpsed the great ocean, you know your own significance and I speak to you of great principles: dimensions are limitless; time is endless; conditions are not invariable; terms are not final. ..."

The world-of-ideas is very real to us, just as real as the well to the well-frog. Our belief that the "well" represents the ocean is the illusion. And so long as we believe that we can learn something about the vast tides of cosmic life, something about the infinite expanse and depths, the great power and wisdom of the ocean by a scientific examination of the well we are perpetuating the illusion.

We will discover more about the well of rational consciousness but like the well-frog we go around and around in an endless circle, unable to escape the hard walls of our prison. Progress can be made only by setting out in a new direction, which is upward. And if we succeed in getting out of the well we shall find ourselves in a larger world of radiant wisdom where the scientific knowledge of our former prison is valueless, for here "dimensions are limitless, time is endless, conditions are not invariable, terms are not final."

Our upward progress out of the darkness is a movement in a figurative sense only, for the dungeons we now inhabit are the intellectual worlds we have created out of the materials of thought. These are the worlds we must reject—nay, destroy—if we hope to achieve a higher form of consciousness.

A partial destruction of these imaginary worlds avails little; we cannot set some ideas aside as false, holding others to be true. This is no more than we have always done, but the process has not brought emancipation. We must try another method—one advocated in all the four-dimensional teachings of the race—one that is epitomized in the cryptic words of Jesus, "There shall not be left here one stone upon another that shall not be thrown down."

This is a psychological necessity, a condition imposed upon us by the very nature of consciousness, yet the distinction is so subtle and elusive that the teachings of the great avatars go unheeded century after century. It is subtle and elusive because we are rational beings. We live among and deal with other rational beings in a world where rationalism is the great virtue; where we take great pride in the logicality of our viewpoints and worship scientific methods. We are enveloped in a cloud of three-dimensionalism, steeped in rational habits and logical traditions. And our intellectual faculties justify it all, seek to maintain the status quo, because it is their province to do so.

Yet the Soul is ever calling us higher, leading us into experiences which show us the ineffectiveness of reason and the illusoriness of factual knowledge. We are not compelled to get out of the "well"; if we elect we can ignore these counter-rational realizations, becoming ever more intellectual and thus less sensitive to the intuitive voice of the Soul. We then move forward, but into a region which Jesus so graphically described as the "outer darkness."

If we determine to escape the limitations of rational consciousness, the "Battle of Armageddon" is inescapable, for both reason and the race-consciousness act as deterrents. It is indeed a period of "tribulation and travail" for the battle is waged alone in the depths of mind and heart. Social existence demands that we maintain some semblance of rationality but inwardly we must strive for total emancipation, wielding the "flaming sword" with a ruthless hand.

Knowledge can no longer be justified by its reasonableness, by its obviousness, or by a weight of scientific evidence; always we must seek the Real—for a realization of that which is now hidden from us by the intellect itself.

21

TRANSCENDING KNOWLEDGE

"THE MIND IS THE SLAYER of the real; let the disciple slay the slayer." So begins the *Voice of the Silence*. In the same book we find another statement, the essence of which is familiar: "The pupil must regain the child state he has lost ere the first sound can fall upon his ear." We must "again become as little children" as Jesus phrased it.

This questioning, wondering, humble state of mind is absolutely essential for the truth-seeker. This kind of humbleness is a sincere acknowledgment of ignorance regarding the world, the laws of life, the purpose of existence, the nature of God. A superficial acknowledgment of ignorance avails nothing; the entire inner attitude must change. As Ouspensky observed, *this* world must become *unreal* before we can perceive the *reality* of *that* world.

The full significance of our task becomes apparent when we realize that our most sacred and idealistic concepts are the products of rationalism, or to state it more directly, when we realize that our concepts of deity cannot be true. Our religious convictions are often so deep-rooted that it is difficult for us to realize that they are rational concepts. In tampering with them, questioning their validity, it seems that we are going too far; but until the prayer of the heart issues forth in the cry, "Oh God, *what* are Thou?" we are not on the straight and narrow pathway that leads to illumination.

Sooner or later Reality answers such prayer by revealing itself, but there is no room for it in the mind crowded with dualistic opinions of good and evil, i.e., with imaginative beliefs which are accepted as real. This is symbolically illustrated in the story of Jesus' nativity. The birth of truth could not take place in the crowded city; but away from the multitude of opposing ideas it occurs in the comparative quiet of a deserted stable, the "stable" signifying a humble mind.

The distinction I am trying to make here is perhaps the most perplexing one that faces us. There is no possibility whatever of achieving Cosmic Consciousness without an intense desire to know the unknown. It makes not the slightest difference what we call the unknown—God, Nature, the Soul, Christ, Reality—but it cannot be discovered so long as we believe we know what it is. It matters little how broad our concepts might be or how much we worship our ideal, spiritual discernment ends the moment we come to believe that we know what God is, what his purpose is, or how he manifests.

Reason tells us that only a primitive mind worships the unknown, but if we remember that this unknown is infinite we will see that a very primitive religious attitude is demanded. It is indeed difficult for us to "regain the childlike state we have lost" but it is nonetheless imperative. It is not belief that we need; we have too much already. We need more un-belief and a greater desire to know. This is the mystic attitude without which illumination is impossible.

There is a popular notion that science and religion are at last beginning to meet on common ground. In one sense of the word this is so, for many of our religious leaders are trying to make religion fit the scientific mold. This does not exalt science, for science itself is unconcerned about the matter. But it does abase religion. It is the province of religion to lead mankind beyond science—to induce the mystic attitude which is the antithesis of our present scientific attitude of mind.

This mystic attitude is primarily a wondering, questioning curiosity regarding the unknown cause of being. Rational explanations cannot satisfy this hunger. There is an unrelenting search for that which antecedes phenomena and ideas.

This is the state of mind which the great religious doctrines seek to inculcate. These doctrines do not claim to reveal the truth; they point out the difference between truth and knowledge, indicate the path which leads to truth, and urge men to follow it. Yet there are always "false prophets"— spiritual leaders who claim to have the truth, and those who try to make religion a plaything of the intellect. In all of the original teachings we find passages which warn us against the spiritual leaders who preach a rational approach to God. The one recorded in the New Testament, is typical:

"Then if any man shall say unto you, lo, here is Christ, or there, believe it not. For there shall arise false Christs and false prophets, who shall show great signs and wonders, insomuch that were it possible they shall deceive the very elect. Behold, I have told you before:

"Wherefore, if they shall say to you, behold, he is in the desert, go not forth: behold, he is in the secret chambers; believe it not. For as the lightning cometh out of the east and shineth even unto the west, so shall also the coming of the Son of man be."

This particular discourse ends by affirming that the "coming of the Son of man" is fulfilled in each generation. But just when it will come for those who are on the path no man knoweth. The word Christ refers to the Soul, or to the

Christ Mind if we prefer the term. The names we use are of little moment, but that which comes unannounced, lighting the heavens with unbelievable radiance, is the realization of Cosmic Being.

This realization cannot be achieved by intellectual methods or through a rational approach. Gautama, the Buddha, made this point even clearer than did Jesus. "Nor sacrifice, nor Vedas, alms, nor works, nor sharp austerity, nor deep study, can win the vision of this form for man." But if we press on day after day in a relentless quest for Reality, discarding factual knowledge and rational hypotheses, we will one day stand face to face with the Soul. And we will then discover that it is unlike anything we have imagined about it, for it is infinite.

In all the Bibles of the race we find the same message: It is reason which must be overcome before we can progress to a higher state. In some of the ancient writings the terms reason and ignorance are synonymous, since the conclusions derived from the evidence of the five senses cannot be true. In the Upanishads it is stated thus:

"Wide apart and leading to different points are these two, ignorance and wisdom.... Fools dwelling in darkness, wise in their own conceit, go round and round, staggering to and fro, like blind men led by the blind. The other world never rises before the eyes of the careless child, deluded by the illusion of wealth. 'This is the world,' he thinks, 'there is no other'—thus he falls again and again under my sway. (The sway of death.)

"The wise man who knows the Self as bodiless within the bodies, as unchanging among changing things, as great and omnipresent, does never grieve. That Self cannot be gained by the Vedas, nor by understanding, nor by much learning. He who has not first turned away from sickness (ignorance or reason) can never attain that Self."

In the Vishnu Purana we find the same undeviating principle: "Having investigated the three worlds and the three kinds of worldly pain, and having acquired detachment from worldly things (racial beliefs) the wise man obtains final liberation. The wisdom—perfect, pure, supreme, undefiled—and the only one by which He is contemplated and known, that is wisdom; all else is ignorance."

Sri Ramakrishna, one of the great religious teachers in India, states it even more concisely: "So long as one does not become simple like a child, one does not get divine illumination. Forget all the worldly knowledge that thou hast acquired and become as ignorant as a little child, and then thou wilt get divine wisdom."

A most unusual statement of this unvarying requisite is found in the Tao-Te-Ching, one of the books of the Taoist scriptures:

Not knowing that one knows is best;

Thinking that one knows when one does not know is sickness;

The sage is never sick; because he is sick of this sickness, therefore he is not sick.

In the Bhagavad-Gita the nomenclature differs but the esoteric message is the same: "The indestructible, the supreme is the Eternal; his essential nature is called Self-knowledge. It is said that the senses are great; greater than the senses is the mind, greater than the mind is the reason, but what is greater than the reason is the Eternal. He who thinketh upon the Ancient, the Omniscient, the All-ruler minuter than the minute, greater than the great, supporter of all, of form unimaginable, refulgent as the sun beyond the darkness, he goeth to the Spirit Supreme, divine."

Here we have one of the most comprehensive statements regarding the novitiate's attitude, yet a careful reading is necessary if we would grasp the meaning. The first part is in reference to the four worlds of Being: the senses, the subjective mind, the reason, and the Eternal or Cosmic Consciousness. The second part indicates that we must go beyond the conceptual limits of the reasoning mind, seeking the meaning of infinity.

It is true that we are science-minded, and that we still hope to reason our way out of the darkness. This is still the mass-attitude, but today there are countless men and women who are seeking a new religion—who are searching for something more dependable than reason, who demand something more satisfying than the cold hypotheses of science and the formalized concepts of the church. This is evidenced by the rapid growth of cults which give new interpretations to the old doctrines, by the great interest in the development of psychic powers, by the wholesale interest in faith cures, and the widespread demand for esoteric literature.

All of these things indicate that there is a growing movement away from rationalism, that a very large number of men and women have already set out in a new direction. It may well be that mankind has reached a point where the transition will occur on a grand scale, but it cannot be a mass movement. In the past humanity has been subject to generic movements, but having achieved individuality our movements henceforth must be specific. Conditions may favor a general movement, but individually we must choose the path we would follow.

If we choose the straight and narrow path which leads quickly to emancipation from the world of conflicting opposites we must of necessity cultivate the mystical attitude of mind. We must realize that there are three kinds of ignorance: pre-scientific, scientific, and mystical, but that only the latter can lead to illumination.

The practice of meditation, or the cultivation of the meditative attitude, is naturally essential; it is in fact synonymous with what I call the mystical attitude. But as I have also indicated it is not an affirmative state of mind which deals with words, or the positive statement of ideas. It is a more or less continuous state of wonderment, an ever-questioning attitude which demands truth and refuses to be satisfied with less.

Of what value, asked an ancient Tibetan Lama, is further reasoning? We cannot arrive at truth by dealing with statements of un-truth. "Although a cloth be washed a hundred times, how can it be rendered clean and pure if it be washed in water that is dirty?" This is the essence of the whole matter, and the measuring-rod by which we gauge our own thinking as we cultivate the mystical attitude.

The "way" is not always light. There will be periods of doubt and depression, times when it appears that the "world" is right and we are wrong. There will be other moments of partial illumination, of amazing realizations and seeming miracles. There will be sacrifice, a sense of loss and loneliness as we discard cherished ideals, but dark as the way must seem at times it is nevertheless the pathway to a freedom of a new order and a magic "password" which gives us entry to the secrets of eternity. This is the great freedom proclaimed by Carpenter in his mystic poem *Toward Democracy*, this democracy being the long heralded 'brotherhood of man' which will be achieved by a transition to a higher form of consciousness.

Freedom at last!

Long sought, long prayed for—ages and ages long;

The burden to which I continually return, seated here thick-booted and obvious, yet dead and buried and passed into a heaven unsearchable; (How know you indeed but what I have passed into you?)

I arise out of the dewy night and shake my wings.

Tears and lamentations are no more. Life and death lie stretched below me. I breathe the sweet ether blowing of the breath of God.

Deep as the universe is my life—and I know it; nothing can dislodge the knowledge of it; nothing can destroy, nothing can harm me.

Joy, joy arise—I arise. The sun darts overpowering piercing rays of joy through me, the night radiates it from me.

I take wings through the night and pass through all the wildernesses of the world and the old dark hold of tears and death—and return with laughter, laughter, laughter;

Sailing through the starlit spaces on outspread wings, we two, O Laughter! Laughter! Laughter!

Freedom! The deep breath! The word heard centuries and centuries beforehand! The Soul singing low and passionate to itself: Joy! Joy!

Not as in a dream. The earth remains and daily life remains, and the scrubbing of doorsteps, and the house and the care of the house remain; but joy fills it; fills the house full of swells to the sky and reaches to the stars: all Joy!

O Freed Soul! Soul that has completed its relation to the body! O soaring, happy beyond words, into other realms passing, salutations to you, freed, redeemed Soul!

What is certain and not this? What is solid?—the rocks?
the mountains? destiny? The gates are thrown wide
open all through the universe. I go to and fro—through
the heights and the depths I go and return; all is well.

Here into this ocean, everything debouches; all interests in
life begin anew. The plantain in the croft looks different
from what it did before.

Do you understand? To realize Freedom or Equality (for
it comes to the same thing) for this hitherto, for you,
the universe has rolled; for this your life, possibly many
lives; for this death, many deaths; for this desires, fears,
complications, bewilderments, sufferings, hope, regret—
all falling away at last duly before the Soul, before You
(O Laughter!) arising the full-grown lover, possessor of
the password.

. . . .

Oh Laughter! The Soul invading, looking proudly upon
its new kingdom, possessing the offerings of all pleasures,
forbidden and unforbidden, from all created things—if
perchance it will stoop to accept them; the everlasting life.

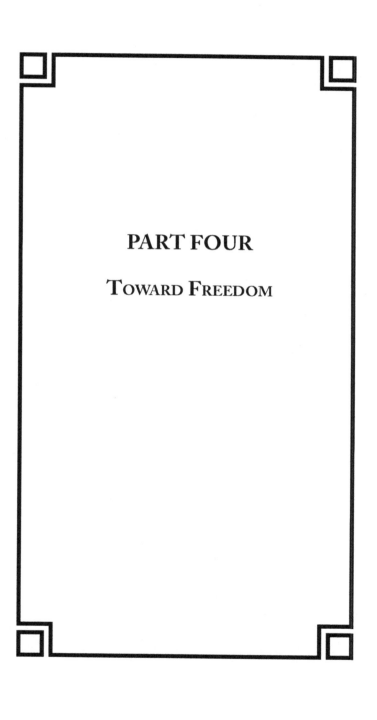

PART FOUR

TOWARD FREEDOM

22

THE ONE GREAT NEED

SPECIFICALLY, HOW DOES ONE BEGIN this quest for Reality? Is there a method or system we can adopt which will enable us to achieve Cosmic Consciousness quickly and without loss of effort? These or similar questions are bound to arise in the minds of sincere truth-seekers, for it seems that our progress would be accelerated if we knew just what to do and how to do it.

In the strictest sense the very nature of the quest prohibits the adoption of a specific system. Methods, forms, systems belong to and are inherent in our present form of consciousness; they are the products of reason, and the instruments which make rational action possible. While we cannot fully emancipate ourselves from the conditions and limitations of rational consciousness at once, we must nevertheless adopt a mode of life which is in keeping with the principles of Cosmic Consciousness.

In various ways I have tried to show that the wisdom of the Soul cannot be logical, and that until we comprehend the meaning of infinity the logic of the Soul will often appear counter-rational and it will always be super-rational. This means that it cannot be circumscribed by rational systems, and that if we attempt to follow the promptings of the Soul the habitual methodicalness of existence must give way to a new spontaneity of action.

There is no especial virtue in trying to be different just to express a disregard for conventions, but it is obvious that we cannot follow the traditional path of racial experience. We must find a different path, one which leads away from reasoned action and toward a more spontaneous life.

There are several reasons why this way of life is known as a "secret path," but the chief one is that it cannot be known intellectually. We cannot plan the journey nor forecast tomorrow's needs. The way is known only to the Soul and it knows the way because it *is* the way. It is cause, and in its infinite wisdom are to be found both the needs and the experiences which will bring emancipation quickly and without loss of effort. The requirements are simple enough: That we keep our minds attuned to the Soul and follow its promptings regardless of the apparent reasonableness of our actions. Every experience, every person, event, word, idea, realization which can in any way contribute to emancipation will appear in its perfectly appointed place and none can be missed. This will not always appear to be true. So often it seems that we are wandering through the darkness alone, that our days are uneventful and profitless; we seem to be getting nowhere, for light does not appear.

I recall such days, many of them, when there seemed to be no progress, or when I seemed to become more hopelessly lost in the muddy waters of speculation. I knew not where I was going or whether there was a Soul; certainly it seemed there was a Soul; certainly it seemed that I was without guidance of any sort. Even after hearing the voice that night in the mountains I did not realize that that which spoke was part of my own being—an integral, supernal part with which I was inseparably unified.

This was not even clear to me during or after the vision in which I saw men and women struggling in the mists of self-consciousness, each going his own way unmindful of the others, each unaware of the "lines of force" which connected him or her with 'something higher'.

The 'something higher' appeared as an external power—infinitely wise, timeless—but nevertheless a power apart from one's being. Even the significance of the vision was soon lost, for again I struggled through the darkness believing I was alone, battling against unknown forces to win I knew not what.

Immersed in this sea of darkness I grasped at every straw that offered a ray of hope. These seemingly vagrant "straws" however, were not the products of reason, for I had long since passed beyond the point where I could accept any rational conclusion. Without exception they were events, words, experiences which strengthened my faith in the existence of Reality. Reality itself was more elusive than ever. I did not know whether it was some form of life, whether it might be an intelligence, an invisible spiritual force, a great power, a law, a person: of its nature I was wholly ignorant, but of its existence I became more and more certain.

I do not mean to say that this certainty was continuous, for there were many times when I doubted the existence of Reality. Yet always during such moments there arrived some minor experience that not only restored my faith, but increased it. Sometimes these experiences were very simple—a recollection of something I had previously read or seen or heard which indicated the reality of Reality. Often it was a passage of scripture that restored my faith—a passage which sometimes seemed to force itself to my attention, revealing a hidden meaning. Perhaps it was the faith of another person, either friend or stranger, this faith not necessarily being a faith in God but simply a belief in the goodness or rightness of life.

Sometimes I was directed into rather unusual situations and the experiences were not always pleasant, but in the end there was always a message of some sort. I experienced this renewal of faith in such subtle ways that I cannot recount them, for as a rule the significance was contained in the experiences themselves and would have little meaning for another person.

There are three things, however, which I recall with undimmed clarity, and they do have significance for everyone who is on the pathway. First, the morning I awoke to a realization of cosmic rhythm, and some time before I "crossed the mystic threshold" I acquired an inward vision which permitted me to *see* noumena; instead of merely thinking, of being conscious of ideas, I perceived them objectively. Specifically I saw portions of my past life, especially of the immediate past, though the ability to see in this manner increased quite rapidly until I perceived larger portions and finally the whole. These noumena appeared to be nothing but mental pictures at first, except that I did not review them in retrospect. I saw them much as one sees pictures projected on a screen.

I had no control over the phenomenon; the various segments of my life seemed to come and go of their own volition. They appeared as momentary flashes, yet all the details were amazingly clear. The various incidents of these segments were apparently unrelated except that each segment seemed to represent a specific period of time; that is, the significance of particular incidents was lost or absorbed by the larger categories which soon began to disclose new meanings. A series of minor incidents seemed to be unified to achieve a net result. Then I began to see a pattern, though the very word may be misleading, for this was not a lifeless pattern; it was a living picture which consisted of my own experiences—pieces of my life, linked together by some invisible force.

At length I perceived the truth: All these experiences existed in some incomprehensible manner before I experienced them, and they existed as living realities now, for I was looking at them. They were in fact part of my own being in the same sense that hands and feet are integral parts, and this suddenly acquired capacity of seeing within myself revealed them to me.

Becoming partially sensitive to this invisible section of being I was able to examine some of the mysteries which are inherent and natural in that section. Thus I came to know that all of my experiences, both pleasant and painful, had been unavoidable—that I could not have missed one experience which contributed to this moment. In what form these experiences existed before their manifestation, and how they were called forth, I did not know at the time. But I did know that experiences are inseparable from being, that they do not develop out of the materials of environment, but out of the materials of the Soul. Moreover, I saw that the true purpose of any experience might be, and most often is, entirely different from what we suppose, for the real purpose is hidden from the intellect because of its inability to comprehend cause.

It was not until complete integration of being had been effected and I had acquired the unrestricted use of the intuitive faculties that I learned the "where" and "how" of these things. Then came the second realization which far transcended the first, for I now discovered the source, or the essence from which these experiences emanated. This essence I have spoken of in various ways—Reality, 'truth', Christ, the 'cosmic wisdom', the 'fourth part of Being', the Soul. I prefer the latter term, but I have found it generally unacceptable, for to many people it means the subjective mind, or the emotional nature.

The real nature of the Soul cannot be defined since it is infinite, but as I use the word it refers to that something other which Jesus called the Father; which Hindus called Brahman; which earlier avatars called Mazda, Lord; and which initiates like Carpenter, Kabir, Whitman have termed Friend or Lover.

Irrespective of name it is Cause, the Originator; it is not born, it does not die; it is omniscient, all-inclusive. It is the *reality* of Being. The realization of which I now speak was the recognition of the unity which had always existed. I discovered that the Soul is not an external something—there is no "being" except for the Soul, no existence apart from it. It is both within and without; it is present in every moment, every event. From its infinite depths come all effects: out of its wisdom are born all experiences, yet in one sense of the word they are not born, for they already exist. All potentialities, all possible relationships, all circumstances and realizations, exist as living realities in its infinite wisdom.

The third realization was that I had called forth certain of these infinite possibilities, and they manifested for me as experiences. I had not "created" a single condition by my thinking, but my *needs* brought them forth and made it possible for them to be experienced. It was a profound and startling realization, very simple in essence, but exceedingly difficult to explain. I knew why Jesus had said, "The Father knoweth what things you have need of, before you ask him." The need itself is the magnet which draws the necessary experience forth. Between the self and the Soul there is a continuous, reciprocating action, and the need is always compensated or fulfilled by experience. Thus the Soul is the "well of living water" which contains all that we can ever know or experience, and the experiences themselves are now living realities, having their existence in the mysterious realm of cause, the fourth side of Being.

Our experiences are therefore determined by our needs, and strictly speaking our needs and our experiences are one and the same; or perhaps it is better to say that they are two aspects of the same thing. Regardless of how we try to express the relationship, our needs are known to the Soul, for the needs themselves originate in the Soul. The Soul is the realm of cause, and the only realm where origination is possible.

Why, then, do we seem to have so many unfilled needs? It is because we do not understand the purport of experience. A need persists day after day, and often year after year, because so many separate experiences are required to bring the realization of fulfillment. The realization of fulfillment is often other than we expect, since it is the cosmic purpose which is being fulfilled.

In Part One it was affirmed that the real purpose of life is to live, to express the infinite livingness of life. This it does through its various members or instruments. Each of us is an instrument, but as three-dimensional instruments we are living below our capacities. The cosmic purpose therefore cannot be measured by our customary conception of "needs." Our great, overall need is to grow up, to achieve the full stature of Being, and every specific need is impregnated with this purpose; every experience tends to bring about a realization of incompleteness.

Thus it is that our needs are endless, and that so many seem to remain unfilled. Countless illnesses, "accidents," losses, disappointments are necessary to make us realize the great need. But once it is realized the very nature of experience is altered and this alteration is effected by the Soul. We now feel the need for truth instead of knowledge; we long for reality in place of illusion. And whereas before our experiences led to the realization of incompleteness they now lead toward the realization of cosmic Being.

If desire is strong, if the realization of our great need is sufficient, we move swiftly to the fulfillment of our destinies. We become more and more sensitive to the results of experience, and realizations follow each other in quick succession. A single event, a minor circumstance, a momentary contact with another person, a bit of scripture may carry us further than a thousand experiences of the old life.

It is because of these things that methods or systems are incompatible with the new life. A method or a practice may be valuable for the moment but all experience now tends to lead us away from rational modes and instruments, making us ever more dependent upon the infinite, super-rational Soul. This is the very essence of Jesus' teaching and the reason why he held the scribes and Pharisees in such disregard, for they typified the men and women who hoped to find salvation in the law—in traditional knowledge, rational conduct, religious dogma.

When we seriously undertake the destruction of our habitual thought-patterns, turning away from the world in search of an incontrovertible reality, our experiences will not always appear orderly and sequential; the results will often seem illogical and thus life itself may seem to be chaotic. Subsequent illumination reveals the marvelous order of this seeming chaos, and we see that we have come by the shortest path. We see also that we have never been alone, but that all action between self and Soul is reciprocal; i.e., that the path was straight so long as the passion for truth did not wane.

It is this—the growing demand for truth, a desire to rend the veil of nescience—which is man's savior. It is this which calls forth the experiences which lead to swift and total emancipation, unlocking secret doors of consciousness which reveal the infinite world of the wondrous.

We can, it says in effect, comprehend the meaning of "small" and "great," but there is an eternal something which is beyond either, and it is this ancient mystery which should hold our attention. Reason tells us that we are separate beings, related to our environment only by accident; but here a counter-rational truth is implied by the words "supporter of all." We perceive "form" everywhere, but this eternal something must have form of a different kind for it is "unimaginable." We believe we live in a world of light, that light being reason; but in contrast to the light of this omniscient wisdom our so-called light is darkness. Last but not least, it is those who think upon these incomprehensible mysteries that achieve union with the Soul.

This longing to know the Infinite, this passion for the super-rational truth, is the mystical attitude which Jesus characterized as humble; it is "meek" in its realization of ignorance; it is "pure" in that it has purged itself of false knowledge; and this "emptiness" of mind is a blessed state, for those who have it shall be filled.

This "ignorance" need not be confessed before men, though some of the great teachers like Socrates have found it expedient to do so. In fact, if one is truly sincere it cannot be confessed; this is a matter which can be shared only with the Soul. It is in the "secret place," or the "closet of the heart" that the change must be wrought.

True worship, then, cannot be defined by a reverence we have for our rational concepts of deity, whether these concepts concern a man crucified, a benign ruler of Heaven, a complex system of natural and spiritual laws, or a combination of all three. To worship "in spirit and in truth" we must set aside all pre-conceived notions, all traditional beliefs, all known facts. We must cultivate the mystical attitude which is defined by a passion for truth, a one-pointed desire to fathom the unknown.

23

DETACHMENT OF THE SELF FROM THE INTELLECT

WHILE THE SECRET PATH leads toward a more spontaneous life this certainly does not imply an emotional or "thoughtless" existence. On the other hand it demands a more intense consciousness of one's inner life, a super-critical examination of one's thoughts, actions, emotions. It demands a relentless questioning of one's motives, of the source and purpose of one's desires. This kind of mental action cannot be called disciplinary, for unless it is spontaneous, arising from a consuming urge to know the truth, it cannot emancipate us from the illusions created and perpetuated by the mind.

There are certain age-old practices which may be called "instruments of delivery" for they are the tools by which emancipation is achieved. They are meditation, contemplation, prayer and action. To become an adept in the use of these instruments requires practice. But the point which I have tried to stress is that these practices must not be relegated to certain periods of the day; they must not become a method which can be picked up or laid aside as one does a book. On the other hand, once the principles are understood they must become the way of life. One's needs will determine the proper instrument, but there will be few moments when one or the other cannot be utilized.

Perhaps there is nothing new or intriguing in the names of these instruments, but I shall try to show that there is something new about them, especially if we learn to use them naturally and spontaneously. Contemplation, for instance, is the most difficult of all instruments to master if we approach it from the orthodox standpoint, for it demands great concentration. Actually it is made possible by the simple expedient of detachment, which in itself is a conscious distinction between that which thinks, the knower, and the elements of consciousness, which are thoughts and emotions. It is imperative that we make this distinction, for until we do we have not learned the simplest fact of self-existence.

Without knowing it we are slaves to our thoughts, and few of us realize how shallow and chaotic our thinking really is. As a rule it is desultory, jumping hither and yon in response to the interests of the senses. We worry and hurry, giving way to impatience, mental fault-finding, wishes and regrets; we engage in mental arguments over imaginary slights, injustices and the like; we spend a lot of energy in the condemnation of self, the world, others; we give undue consideration to trifles, stewing over conditions which are beyond our control; we fear the results of action and also the results of inaction, making decisions only to remake them; we anticipate loss and pain and disappointment; we pinch off a bit of this and that, mulling over these inconsequential bits of nothing until the senses take us elsewhere.

Sprinkled in with these aimless, fear-saturated thoughts are others of a more pleasant nature to be sure. We plan and hope and love; we give some thought to our ambitions, our loved ones, our aspirations; we concentrate on the work at hand and try to find better ways of doing things; we give a moment or two to devotion, praise, or prayer; we dream a little and occasionally we become absorbed in the contemplation of beauty. But throughout all of this we are relatively helpless prisoners, unable to distinguish between self and the rabble of conflicting thoughts and emotions which surround and control us.

This may seem to be an exaggerated picture and in some cases it may be, but on the whole it is rather an accurate summary of what takes place in the average rational mind. Let us draw aside for one day, watching the thoughts which occupy the mind; if we do this for one day, or for a few moments each day for a week, the revelation may be astonishing. We will find that what we call reason is little more than a hodge-podge of chaotic thoughts, and that we are their subjects and vassals rather than the reverse.

How helpless we are amidst this rabble is demonstrated almost every day of our lives. A thought of some impending calamity, of an unpleasant but unavoidable experience which awaits us, or the fear of some possible loss takes possession of the mind; we do not question its right to be there, its right to make us miserable and non-effective. We let it go and come as it will, weaving a dark and sinister pattern as it circles and spins about, until the whole attitude of mind is colored by its unwelcome presence.

Day after day we let our thoughts drive us in a vicious cycle of hurry, believing that the mad rush represents vitality and progress. We pride ourselves on the diversity and scope of our activities, little realizing that it is our thoughts which hold the whip—that we are not free men and women but creatures hounded by the "bat-winged phantoms which flit through the corridors of the brain."

We say that every man and woman has the right to think as he or she chooses. We do have the right, but we do not exercise it. Thought control is practically unknown, and for that matter almost unimaginable. It is true that many of us have made a start in this direction by devoting a few moments a day to meditation. Such practices may be beneficial, but the secret of mind control lies in what Gautama called *detachment.*

I have already indicated the nature of detachment, for it is not a detachment from things so much as it is an aloofness from the thought-machine. We stand aside as it were and look into our own minds. For a moment or two we look at ourselves in an effort to discover the nature of the thoughts and emotions which occupy the attention.

This sort of detachment is not difficult to achieve, though at first it may be somewhat fleeting. Recognizing self as an entity, or as the knower, one withdraws from the center of the mind, looking down on the mental activity as a spectator. Not critically, but with intense curiosity. For if we begin immediately to criticize, it will be impossible to achieve detachment. Curiosity is the key, and discrimination is the thing to be avoided. The intellect is the discriminating instrument, and here we are seeking to rise above the intellect, if only for a moment.

The power of withdrawing from the center of mental activity will increase with a little practice, and the experience will disclose the amazing difference between the "cupful of reality" which we call Self, and the ideas about self and the world which pass for reality.

This detachment of self from the intellect opens up new fields of experience, for we become increasingly aware of the illusions which have enslaved us, and in becoming aware of them the illusion vanishes. Detachment opens the "eye of the Soul" and permits us to see without the aid of the mind or the physical eyes. In other words it makes intuitive perception possible, which perception is wholly independent of thoughts.

This sort of detachment must not be confused with self-analysis—it is not an examination of past actions. It is not a process of thinking at all. One becomes aware of the mental processes, emotions and reactions, with a growing desire to understand them. This is the one thing we have not tried to do: we have rationalized and analyzed our desires and actions, have tried to overcome negative thinking by positive thinking, but we have never examined the whole process in an effort to understand the nature of thought. This kind of examination must of necessity be non-discriminating; it must be as vitally interested in negative or evil thoughts as it is in positive or good thoughts. Instead of seeking to cover up or hide the cause of evil thinking by rationalizing or by substitution, we must try to find the cause. This we cannot do through analysis, for the mind is self-deluding. Analysis requires discrimination, the recognition of opposites and the necessity of choice. Thus analysis always produces conclusions, which are not synonymous with understanding.

If we would understand the mind and thus discover the basic cause of illusions we must rise above the mind with its constant discriminations. We must make an effort to see it in its totality, to be as vitally interested in its evils, fears, deceptions, pains, hatreds, as in their opposites. We must want to know *why* we fear and love, and *how* the mind works to produce its illusions. Instead of seeking escape from evil thinking, from the moods of despondency and mental conflict, we must seek an understanding of the whole process of thought. This cannot be achieved through substitution, for then we are merely running away. It cannot be achieved through analysis, for then we are not only utilizing opposites, but dealing with past actions in an effort to set up a new pattern for future actions. The new patterns may appear better, but they are nevertheless constricting and in time will become prisons. If we would escape the prisons produced by our thinking we must detach ourselves from the instrument which produces them. Without discrimination, without analysis and without mental effort, we must begin to observe the mind in action, inspired only by a desire to understand.

A desire such as this does not, cannot, seek to change things. On the other hand it must discover the meaning of fear, of suffering and thus it watches, observes, but does not draw conclusions. For the intuitive understanding which comes as a result of this kind of intense, whole-hearted observation is unlike our rational conclusions.

The word "detachment" may be somewhat misleading, for as it is used here it does not imply a lethargic impersonalness, or non-interest. The detachment is from the mind, or from the illusion that consciousness depends upon thought. In reality it connotes a heightened self-consciousness, but not simply an intensification of our present form of consciousness. Rising above the mind we become aware of the mind in action, suffering with its conflicts, but at the same time trying to understand the cause of conflict. This, as I have stated, cannot be ascertained by analysis—by more thinking—but only through a movement which emancipates us from the hypnotic slumber of mind-consciousness.

Detachment makes us spectators, self-observers, seekers of understanding, but does not free us from the pain and

conflict produced by the mind. Actually the pain and conflict will be heightened, for now we are trying to understand
the mystery of cause and this very effort produces pain.
Moreover, as we begin to perceive the illusoriness of our
mental world, the shallowness and ineffectiveness of our
thinking, the poignancy of suffering increases. But out of
this travail will be born a new and different kind of understanding—one which liberates us forever from the fearful
illusion of rational consciousness.

The process of detachment is hard to describe; it cannot
be reduced to a system or method, since its very purpose is to
take us beyond reason, to a state of spontaneous contemplation. Yet if there is a heartfelt desire to know the meaning
of life, a growing demand for reality, and a willingness to
understand life regardless of the cost of mental suffering,
there is little need for specific instructions. The Soul knows
the way and will provide the necessary experiences.

24

THE MYSTICAL ATTITUDE

"DIALECTIC," SAID PLATO in his *Republic,* "and dialectic alone, goes directly to the First Principles and is the only science which does away with hypotheses in order to make her ground secure." According to the Socratic philosophy, science and human knowledge have their places in the life of mankind, illusory though they be. Science is the vehicle for the "production, construction, and protection" of the things which make human society possible. But the so-called laws upon which these sciences are based are merely hypotheses—they are not universal principles and science itself is not interested in discovering the principles. All of these hypotheses (which are accepted as true principles by the majority of mankind) together with all the products of science, lead to greater enslavement unless man discovers their illusory nature.

The true philosopher seeks the real through the painful process of disentanglement, or as Plato variously terms it, conversion, emancipation (circumcision). Coming at last out of the den of rational consciousness one achieves "magnificence of mind and is the spectator of all time and existence." Return to the "den" is necessary, but knowing the real one is never again confused by the "shadows." Having acquired the habit of again seeing in the dark one will "see then a thousand times better than the inhabitants of the den, and will know what the several images are and what they represent."

The meaning of the term *dialectic* is literally the discrimination of truth from error, but as Plato used it, it implies more than the use of logic. Reason, he affirmed, is the instrument we use in tearing down the old structures—the hypotheses and superstitions and conclusions which mankind has so long accepted as true. This enables us to approach the light, but truth itself must be apprehended through the "eye of the Soul." Dialectic, then, involves the use of both reason and intuition.

The manner in which we employ the principles of dialectic is analogous to the manner in which we learned to reason. During the first years of life the earth appeared to be flat and the concept of a globular world was beyond our comprehension. But we had a healthy, open-minded curiosity, and an intense desire to know. Accepting the new concept on faith—as a principle—we slowly destroyed the primitive idea of a flat earth and eventually achieved the adult viewpoint. In short we reasoned from *principle* and against *appearances*.

We followed the same method in acquiring our concepts of a solar system, axial and cyclic motion, etc. It appeared to us that the earth was stationary, that the sun rose and set. At first even the concept of a single sun was incomprehensible, for it seemed to us that a new sun appeared every morning. Accepting the principle of a single sun, turning the strange concept over in the mind, musing about the mystery, trying to eliminate the apparent contradictions, we finally achieved a rational understanding of the matter.

Today these concepts of time and motion are firmly fixed, and we forget that they are concepts. We accept them as incontrovertible facts of nature. Time, we say is a progression, and our units of measurement are certainly real; motion, change, growth are cosmic realities for we experience them as such. This is altogether different from the childish attitude which enabled us to emerge from a more primitive state to mature self-consciousness.

Our ideas of space, time and motion are three-dimensional, and from the cosmic standpoint are just as absurd as our childish ideas of a flat earth and many suns. Progress now depends upon a disbelief in three-dimensional concepts and our desire to rise above them. We must accept certain new principles, reasoning from them and against appearances.

In these studies we have laid a foundation for a potential understanding of cosmic principles. These principles can merely be indicated, and the statements which follow should not be accepted as truth. They are symbols which the mind can get hold of and use as a means to an end, the end being a quickening of intuitive perception.

First: There is within and about us another world. It is similar in its essential nature to the worlds we already know—the world of instinct, the world of emotion, the world of reason. In other words it is a world of consciousness, and the recognition of this new world depends on sensuous perception—additional or extended perception.

Second: While it is similar to the worlds through which we have already progressed, in that it is a realm of consciousness, it is entirely new and different from anything we have known. The faculties, powers, units of mentation and emotions are vastly different, and realizations are absolute instead of relative.

Third: It is a world of infinite magnitudes and unlimited horizons. In this world all motion is internal, for one's consciousness includes all things. Without physical movement one can be in two or more "places" at once; also without effort one may enter the world of the atom or encompass the farthest stars.

Fourth: It is a world of four dimensions, the intuitive faculty revealing the invisible side of all things. This side is the realm of cause, and the cause is not determined nor affected by anything in the phenomenal world; but the phenomena of the three-dimensional world are always determined by the infinite wisdom of the Soul.

Fifth: It is a realm of transcendent logic. In this world opposites do not exist. There is neither good nor evil, end nor beginning. There is on the other hand a perception of unity, resulting in a logic which does not discriminate, reason, or formulate conclusions.

Sixth: It is a realm of transcendent law. Cosmic law is a living power, conscious, super-intelligent, omnipotent. It is a power which has no opposite, thus no limitations of any kind.

Seventh: Cosmic time is an eternal *now*. This *now* is identical with space, in which all things exist eternally. Yesterdays and tomorrows, together with all their events and conditions, exist spatially and can be examined as one examines the pages of a book.

Eighth: Cosmic Consciousness reveals a perfected, non-evolving universe. The changes which we now perceive, and which make it appear that the world is evolving, are due to sensuous limitations. Overcoming these limitations we find that the world is finished, complete, perfect, but that its perfection is vibrantly dynamic, not static.

Ninth: The higher consciousness reveals the living-ness of the world. Nothing is dead, rigid or unconscious.

Everything lives, breathes, is conscious. One life pervades all things.

Tenth: Intuitively one perceives and understands the deepest secret of all, for the Soul-faculties reveal the universe as *person*. The world is a living Being whose form is light, whose power is all-mighty, whose wisdom is infinite. This supernal Being is the source of all works, all lesser forms of intelligence, since it is the Soul of all things. It is in all things yet above all things, radiant, rhythmic, loving, laughing.

Accepting these statements as possibilities, turning them over and over in the mind, meditating on the great mystery of being and the eternalness of all things; musing on the strangeness of cosmic time; pondering the mystery of a power which is not limited by natural laws; attempting to see the hidden side of things; trying to reconcile opposites so that we may grasp the import of cosmic unity; thinking about the Soul, wondering what it is and how it is, longing to know this Reality first-hand, we approach the light.

The purpose of such meditation will be defeated if we attempt to mold these statements into a pattern of thought, if we attempt to construct from them a mental image of the cosmos as we think it should be. The mind will do this the moment it believes it understands the significance of the above statement; it cannot do so as long as there is a question, an unsolved mystery.

What we call understanding is nothing more than the sum of our rational conclusions. When we understand there is no longer any mystery. The reasoning mind cannot tolerate mystery; it must be explained, solved, reduced to a formula. Or, if we cannot solve the mystery we accept a statement about it as true, believing the matter solved by this substitution.

Somewhere in the Hebrew scripture there is a statement to the effect that we can be made whole by the renewing of our minds. The renewing, however, does not consist of our mental acceptance of new ideas; rather it consists of a new attitude of mind, one which is intrigued and baffled by the incomprehensible mystery of life.

The mystery of an infinite universe will always be a mystery, even when we have achieved initiation. The realization of completeness solves all the questions of the intellectual mind, but the mystery of infinity is never solved. There are no limits, no bottom or ceiling, no center or circumference which can circumscribe an infinite consciousness. Though we comprehend the meaning of genesis, of creation, and realize the unity and eternalness of life, it is forever revealing new wonders. There is no satiation, no end to the mystery of a life which is both infinite and eternal. The mind, however, unable to comprehend the infinity in which it is immersed, invents theories which destroy or cover up the great mystery. In doing this the mind creates a false sense of security, for it is afraid of the unknown.

The purpose of meditation is to regain our natural sensitivity to life, to its unfathomable depths. It should lead the mind away from the obvious, away from traditional knowledge and the construction of hypotheses, to an awareness of the baffling mystery which surrounds us. It is this very mystery which must intrigue us—the realization that we do not know. This attitude of bafflement, coupled with a passionate desire to know, is the secret key which unlocks the doors of a vaster consciousness. For out of the pain, the mental anguish, the chaotic darkness which tortures the mind when it realizes that it does not know, is born a new sensitiveness. The old faculties are quickened and new ones are born. One day the travail and suffering is over and we awaken to the realization of a majestic universe, filled with the splendor of divine fire. The old questions and longings are forgotten in the ecstasy of the new freedom.

Meditation is any form of thinking which rises above habitual channels to grapple with a great mystery. Periods of the day which are reserved for meditation have little value; in fact they prolong or intensify the habit-forming tendencies of the rational mind. Invariably they lead to stagnation of thought, to a crystallization of a pattern of thought.

It is from action that an ever-new approach is wrought. Every act, every incident of the daily life is filled with mystery. We know not the life which fashions our bodies, the source of emotion and intelligence, or the meaning of movement. We know not why we eat, the significance of taste, the purpose of food or the secrets of metabolism. We know not whence we came, where we are, what we are. We know not the purpose of ideas and ideals, the manner in which they are born or the substance of which they are made. We cannot comprehend the meaning of diversity in unity. We are unable to grasp the meaning of time and space. We have invented reasonable explanations which temporarily satisfy the intellect, but at the same time we have insulated ourselves against life; we have killed the sense of wonderment without which there can be no psychic growth.

In accepting life as an unknown and unrealized mystery—as something vaster than science and philosophy surmise—and by questioning the meaning and purpose of all things, by demanding to know the source of all things, the mind is renewed. It regains its lost heritage, its spontaneous inquisitiveness, its worship of the unknown and by this very process it is made whole.

Meditation, then, must arise from our actions. It must be spontaneous, the natural result of our longing to know the unknown. Toward this end a statement of principles may serve as reminders, as stepping stones to a realization of mystery; from them we may reason in an effort to overcome the crystallized concepts of intellectualism, but beyond this they have no value. Truth comes not through the acceptance of statements, but through the continual effort of the mind to know the unknown.

25

"A Peace That Passeth All Understanding"

There are certain experiences which demonstrate the illusoriness of time and motion, thereby bringing us close to a perception of the real, but as a rule the experiences themselves are considered illusory. I refer to those rare moments of mental and physical peace during which we lose contact with the objective world. They might be called periods of involuntary mental repose, or spontaneous contemplation, and they often result from the reading of poetry, absorption in the beauty of a sunset, listening to great music and the like. We are subtly lifted above the world of ant-like activity, and for a few wonderful moments experience an inner stillness and peace. But the hurry and bustle of objective life, we imagine, represent the sphere of reality, and anything which tends to make this confusing maelstrom appear real is itself unreal.

If we accept the premise of an infinite universe we must also accept its correlatives—timelessness and changelessness. We then see that our present realization of life as a bubbling cauldron is a surface illusion, and that these moments of spontaneous contemplation take us toward the depths, where the real nature of being can be discovered and experienced.

We see that our present conceptions of time and motion are unreal, and that the worship of these illusions forces us into channels of objective activity which get us nowhere. Like Chuang's well-frog we go round and round, believing that the little ripples we make in the shallow waters of rational consciousness represent cosmic life, and that this kind of activity is the aim and purpose of the infinite wisdom.

I do not mean to imply that objective activity is unnecessary. This, it seems to me, is the basic error of Hindu philosophy. Realizing that human progress cannot be measured in terms of objective activity, the founders of the ancient wisdom schools leaned over backwards, affirming that the pathway to emancipation was one of inaction. This was not in keeping with the teachings of the great Hindu avatars, for they preached the necessity of action. It is like many of the errors which have crept into Christian philosophies, for while

Jesus recommended the life of action, he affirmed that it must be founded on prayer. In fact he made it clear that prayer is far more important than action, and that it should become so habitual that we "pray without ceasing." But we have leaned too far forward. In the quest for objective knowledge, material possessions and physical pleasures we have neglected the most important thing, which is the mystical attitude.

The mystical attitude may not fit the orthodox conception of prayer, but it is the kind of prayer Jesus advocated. This attitude as I have indicated, must become habitual in order to be effective. We must cultivate a "meekness" of mind, which acknowledges our ignorance regarding the world, self, and God, and at the same time longs for direct contact with the Real. It is by and through such meekness that we "inherit the earth," for sooner or later we are inducted into a realm where unity is realized.

In a subsequent chapter I will indicate more fully the relative balance of "prayer" and "action," and how necessary both are if emancipation is to lead us beyond the semi-trance state so ardently desired by the Eastern novitiate. Here I would simply point out the possibility of utilizing some of the normal experiences which tend to reveal the super-rational truth of being, but which are so often dismissed as illusory and of little significance.

In the contemplation of a work of art, the beauties of nature, the mystic meaning of poetry, the magic power of a great symphony, we are often carried beyond the phenomenal world, and occasionally all awareness of time, self, motion, is lost. During such moments we do not think about the beauty or the mysterious spiritual quality of the phenomenon; we absorb it without discrimination. In other words we become unified with the object or phenomenon, and some part of its invisible nature is apprehended intuitively.

Perhaps there have been days in spring or early summer when we have sensed an unusual kinship for the earth, and divorced from the struggle and incessant activity of normal life we have come en rapport with nature. This feeling of unity sometimes culminates in a state of mental and emotional passivity during which the thought-processes slow down or fade into the background of consciousness. Awareness is acute, but the struggle and bustle of habitual existence seem far-removed and unreal.

Slowly, or sometimes quite suddenly, we become aware of the vital forces of nature, but in an unusual way: we are not actively aware of the particular forms of nature, but of an underlying harmony. Life appears to be the great Reality, but the movement of forms is peaceful, harmonious, and strangely hushed. For an instant the old sense of becoming is replaced by a mystical awareness of being: we sense the perfection of things-as-they-are, and if the experience is deep enough we realize that they have ever been thus—peaceful, harmonious, unhurried, timeless.

Perhaps there have been winter days when the very stillness of a snow-covered landscape quickened within us a mystic sense of reality. In the great silence and utter immobility of all things, we vaguely apprehend a reality which refuses to yield itself completely. Perhaps the unfamiliar shape of familiar objects helps to induce this elusive realization, but it is the stillness of the world which entrances us—which calls to some deeply buried memory of origin—for stillness is characteristic of the absolute.

Occasionally a winter day may appraise us of the reality of life, or the timelessness of life in an altogether different way. Toward spring we may sense the livingness of a "dead" world, a livingness which we cannot see, feel, taste, smell, or hear. Beneath the rigid forms of tree trunks and naked branches, in the brown grass, in the frozen earth we recognize a force which pervades all things—a pulsating breath which ebbs and flows with cosmic rhythm. For endless ages the flow of this breath has been waking the earth, and we know that it will continue to do so for other endless ages. This fleeting sense of continuity may be dissipated almost as soon as it appears, but for an instant we look beneath the appearances and apprehend the eternalness of life.

For many centuries night time and an open fire have been the stimulants of mystical apprehension. Firelight has always held a strange fascination for the mind. The ceaseless "change which does not change" is more clearly represented in the glowing embers than in any other natural

phenomenon. Perhaps we sense the mystery of the generation of life—a living force rising from an unknown source.
At any rate an open fire calls to something deep within
us. The flickering light takes form, ever changing, fluid,
and slowly the fixed patterns of thought respond. A subtle
change in consciousness is induced and without effort we
rise above the objective world.

In such a simple and natural manner we often approach
the realm of Reality. We lapse into a contemplative state
which occasionally is so pure that the thought-machine
ceases to function. We observe, but do not draw conclusions. Withdrawn from the objective world we view the
noumena of the inner world as from a great height, or from
the background of consciousness, and as entities apart from
the world. We are not concerned with the problems of
existence, the questions of the intellect, nor even with the
images which drift through the field of consciousness. We
are disinterested observers, completely satisfied with the
peace and quiet of the moment.

We do not realize how silent, timeless and peaceful existence has been until we shake ourselves and again become
absorbed in the world of particulars. And then the momentary awareness of peace and timelessness is dismissed as an
illusion having no especial importance or significance. So
strong are the bonds of our illusory existence that we discredit the reality of peace even when we experience it.

Yet there are some things which these contemplative
moods reveal, one of which is that time, space and motion—
or our realization of them—depend upon consciousness.
They are not "fixed" phenomena of nature, but are relative
phenomena of consciousness.

The contemplative state, whether it be spontaneous or deliberately induced, always affects our realization of space. Space, let us say, is enlarged when the horizons of the mind recede, whenever we free ourselves from the activities of the thought-machine. If the contemplative state is pure enough all three-dimensional limitations fade away and we find ourselves in a super-sensuous, fluid world.

Time also changes. The pressure which drives us so unmercifully is lifted and we lose track of the movement of time. There is no awareness of the divisions of time, no "before-now-after." All moments are merged into a motionless now which, while we experience it, has neither beginning nor ending.

During the spell of such mystic contemplation the realization of motion undergoes a subtle change. Awareness of objective motion becomes unreal and finally non-existent. Motion is now transferred to noumena, i.e., we perceive the motion of mental images, which seem to float through the mind. And if we press on to a still higher state of contemplation, known in the East as *Samadhi,* we find ourselves immersed in the tranquility of a timeless and motionless world.

Plato's declaration that the hypotheses of science are false is thus substantiated by personal experience; for we see that any theory or statement of a "natural law" which accepts space, time and motion as fixed conditions, i.e., as inherent characteristics of the objective world, cannot be true. We see that the astronomer's concept of a stellar universe measurable by light-years is not commensurate with the universe itself; that the philosophers' belief that the macrocosm is or can be similar to our three-dimensional conception of the microcosm is also erroneous.

From such false readings of nature we cannot discover cosmic purpose, regardless of how perfectly we reason. We cannot find the true answers to such simple questions as, What am I? Why am I here? We must discover the macrocosm first; then we will know the meaning and purpose of the microcosm. But knowing these things we shall still be unable to tell another, for truth is incomprehensible to the intellect. Each man or woman must make the journey alone—must become sensitive to his or her own Soul-faculties, for the infinite can be known only through our cosmic faculties.

While such moods as I have described are more or less involuntary we can profit by them when they do come, for during such moments we are sensitive to the higher faculties. These are the moments which presage a wider, deeper experience, and they should not be dismissed as satisfying though unreal experiences; on the other hand they must be welcomed as indications of spiritual progress, and as such be forced to yield their fullest realizations.

Infrequent as such experiences may have been in the past they will come more often once we recognize their value, since it is the province of experience to lead us toward the realization of infinity. The mystical attitude, or the desire to know the unknown, is undoubtedly the greatest contributing factor in spiritual growth; but the practice of detachment—of withdrawing from the center of mental activity—opens the way for just such experiences as these.

26

INITIATION

ONE OF THE FIRST significant changes which occurs during initiation is an apprehension of a strange new unity with nature. The ordinary sense of separateness, or of personal existence, is replaced by a realization of oneness with all things, or perhaps with some particular part of nature. I have referred to this unity a number of times by saying that one becomes the cosmos, that time and space are annihilated, that one enters the stone, the star, etc. The illusion of duality vanishes completely and is replaced by a realization of cosmic individuality.

In my own case there was the sudden discovery of an amazing kinship with the leaves and flowers of a florist's shop, which expanded the following day until the realization of being was all-inclusive. Jacob Boehme tells of the suddenly acquired faculty of looking into the herbs and grass and reading their innermost secrets. Plotinus said that "When we see God we see him not by reason, but by something that is higher than the reason. It is impossible, however, to say about him who sees, that he *sees*, because he does not behold and discern two different things. He changes completely, ceases to be himself, preserves nothing of his I. Immersed in God, he constitutes one whole with him; like the center of a circle, which coincides with the center of another circle." (Letters to Flaccus.)

In *The Varieties Of Religious Experience,* William James recounts a personal experience which indicates an approach to this unity. "The consciousness of God's nearness came to me sometimes.... . A Presence, I might say ... something in myself made me feel a part of something bigger than I, that was controlling. I felt myself one with the grass, the trees, the birds, insects, everything in nature. I exulted in the mere fact of existence, of being part of it all—the drizzling rain, the shadows of the clouds, the tree-trunks and so on."

This realization of unity is emotional rather than intellectual; one *feels* the unity which the mind cannot comprehend. Not only does this inward state indicate one's nearness to the threshold of Cosmic Consciousness, but it also suggests the manner by which we can approach the mystic door. Obviously it is not by thinking—by an imaginative process. It is made possible by detachment. One must become unknowing and uncritical, passing beyond discrimination to a *receptive* condition of consciousness.

For example, there are two ways of listening to music, and I am referring to the act of attentive listening rather than the mere awareness of music which permits the mind to wander listlessly from one thing to another. In one instance we listen with the objective mind as a critic of composition, technique, rendition, tone, etc.; in other words we discriminate and compare. Perhaps it would be better to say that we listen with analytical minds, for most of us do not profess to be critics. The second way is more impersonal; composition and technique and all the rest are forgotten; we hear the soul-stirring harmonies. We feel the music rather than hear it, i.e., we experience it emotionally.

In the second instance we may know nothing whatever about music from an academic standpoint, yet it lifts us into another world where we discover meanings which do not permit further interpretation. In short, we become sensitive to the kind of emotions which the composer felt, and which he could express through no medium except music. We achieve a mystic blending of self and music which is beyond intellectual appreciation, and which leaves us speechless when the spell is ended.

Listening to great music in this manner is an art which is quickly acquired since it does not demand a knowledge of music. In most cases a total ignorance of music would be beneficial, for too often we try to imagine what the composer meant. A certain amount of mental discipline is necessary, of course, for we must either still the thought-machine or withdraw from it. Awareness must be detached from all save the music, and whenever we achieve this detachment we find that some essential part of being is flowing into the music. It is a reciprocal process, for there is an inflow of music and an outflow of the exalted emotions of the Soul. This is indicative of direct contact with a phenomenon of the objective world—it is intuitive apprehension.

I do not intend to imply that there is any special virtue in music which makes this kind of apprehension possible. I have used music merely as an example. The same kind of unity is possible with nature, or with any aspect of nature, and it is the mystical attitude which makes intuitive apprehension possible.

One's novitiate can be shortened by cultivating the habit of looking at all things with new interest. There is an unscientific, but awe-inspiring mystery concealed in the commonest form; there is an unknown side to every leaf, pebble, cloud, event, person. While we cannot penetrate to the mystery at once we can and do become sensitive to our higher faculties by looking at all things with new purpose.

We are now unified in consciousness with all things, but we are not aware of the unity. We cannot realize this unity by simply declaring it over and over again. Neither can we imagine the realization into existence; this would be the same as imagining new meanings in music. We must try to pass beyond the realm of intellectual appreciation, rising to the unknowing, uncritical area of detachment.

It is the mystery, the unknown, which must intrigue us. In order to even approach this mystery we must first realize that we do not know anything about it, and that the three-dimensional form with which we are so familiar cannot represent the Reality. We have given meanings and purposes to all the objects of our world-images, but these are not cosmic meanings and purposes. To discover the real we must set aside the intellectual concepts and look for the unknown, wondering, intrigued by the possibility of infinity and unity, believing there are meanings and purposes in all things which imagination and reason will never discover.

At first we may be unable to perceive anything unusual in nature and our efforts may even appear absurd, but every effort we make renders the veil of nescience a bit thinner. This questioning attitude of mind cannot be over-emphasized. It must become habitual. Taking nothing for granted because of its familiarity, accepting no rational explanation for the phenomena of life, discounting all accepted theories and beliefs concerning the world, self, God, we must continually look for the mystery which is hidden in the form of things.

Questions relating to self are vital. Who am I? What am I apart from this name, this body, this mind? Why am I here? Where did I come from? Where am I going? What is the purpose of all this struggle? What is behind the curiosity which impels me to ask such questions? Queries of this nature pave the way for direct illumination, for the answer comes to those who are ever seeking, asking, knocking; never to those who think they know.

All preconceived notions must be disregarded when we ask such questions, and all imaginative and speculative answers set aside as quickly as they arise. We must ask with the fore-knowledge that we do not know, and with the realization that only an expansion of consciousness which reveals the infinite can supply the answers.

Such questions as these often help to induce a mood of spontaneous contemplation, which mood is closely related to the natural state of Cosmic Consciousness. Mystery is the key word of Cosmic Consciousness, for as inconsistent as it may appear we are plunged into a sea of eternal mystery when we pass beyond the limits of rational consciousness. Knowing the answers to all questions of the intellect we are increasingly fascinated by the fathomless mystery of all things. In serene contemplation we ponder the great mystery of being; we know what things are, how they are, why they are, but at the same time we marvel.

This sense of wonderment grows rather than diminishes, for it does not result from our sudden induction into the world of infinites. Initiation often produces a sense of skepticism at first, for perception is so utterly different that one is not sure of his sanity. This quickly gives way to a physical, emotional, mental and spiritual ecstasy of realization as one achieves complete unity. Then only does one begin to taste the depths of mystery, and it is a process in which there can be no satiation, no end to the mystic wonder, for the beauty and mystery of the cosmos are infinite.

It is the infinity of things which is the source of never ending wonder, and which drew from one initiate the exclamation that "God himself is immersed in the contemplation of the infinite mystery and beauty of his own nature."

We approach the threshold of Cosmic Consciousness in the degree that we are able to simulate the condition of mind which is natural to that region. This is spontaneous contemplation, and it is made possible through the mystical attitude and detachment.

27

SURRENDER TO THE SOUL

THE LAST AND UNDOUBTEDLY the most formidable obstacle one encounters in the search for Reality is the age-old belief in personal autonomy. Of all human beliefs it is the most sacred and therefore the most difficult to overcome. Intellectually we may be able to accept the basic premise of the 'great doctrine'—that man and the cosmos are one—but we draw back in alarm when we begin to realize the final implication, which is that the cosmos *is* the One.

If there is but one Reality it will be possible to know this Reality only by union with it. It cannot be known objectively at all, for unity precludes the possibility of a consciousness of duality. That is, there could not be a realization of self as an entity apart from the cosmos and at the same time be a realization of oneness. Since the Cosmos is infinite, changeless, absolute, it cannot *become* anything; only man's awareness can change, and thus it follows that personal belief in separateness must be destroyed.

This, of course, has been the message of all great religious teachers and it is especially emphasized in the teachings of Jesus. He affirmed that one must lose one's life in order to experience a larger life, but the statement has long since lost its tremendous significance. As the simplest kind of statement regarding the only reality we know—consciousness—it has been perverted to fit the narrow religious views of many sects, and has meant everything from asceticism to life in a heaven paved with gold.

If we accept the fundamental premise that self and the Cosmos are one we must of necessity accept the Cosmos, its purpose and will as our own. The notion of separate existence, separate purpose and separate responsibilities must be set aside as illusions of an immature form of consciousness. All ideas of self-reliance must give way to utter reliance on the Soul. We must abandon reason as a guide to action and step forth on faith alone, trusting that this final act of renunciation will bring a realization of unity.

Most men and women are willing to meet this demand half-way. There is a willingness to share the responsibility. This attitude is expressed in the popular belief that "man and God work together" in a sort of partnership. Man, of course, is the intelligent half of the firm, for God merely created the desert; "man turned it into a garden."

Even though our concept of deity be more personal the general idea of a partnership is retained. We believe that we have certain responsibilities and also the God-given faculty of reason with which to work out the solutions to our problems. This division of responsibility and labor will not suffice if we hope to bridge the gap in consciousness. There must be a complete and unequivocal rejection of the illusory belief in personal existence, for the idea of personal will is just as erroneous as any other rational conclusion.

Accepting unity as a fact we must put our trust in the Soul, acting on faith alone until we become more sensitive to our intuitive faculties. This means, of course, that personal autonomy must be surrendered, and the Soul must replace the I in our thinking.

According to the Bhagavad-Gita there are two paths to emancipation: one through contemplation and the other through action. To state it more accurately there are two ways of following the same path, for contemplation and action are both necessary. This rule is the same as the one advocated by Jesus: While living in the world, active in the affairs of the world, one may achieve "salvation" through prayer and action. This kind of action, however, is not premeditated; one must take no thought for the morrow, but must rely on the Soul for guidance; believing that we are unified with the Soul, that it is directing our destinies, and that it is the power which doeth the works.

The world, says the Bhagavad-Gita, is bound by action. Whether we will or not we cannot escape action. But unless all actions are performed in a spirit of sacrifice they are not worthy of a man and can lead only to destruction—the destruction being a greater entanglement in the web of nescience with its attendant losses, fears, pains and disappointments.

The kind of sacrifice called for is altogether different from the old Hebrew concept. The Hindu scriptures like the New Testament affirm that we must give up our belief in personal autonomy rather than the fruits of our actions. "The righteous who eat the *remains* of the sacrifice are freed from sin; but the impious who dress food for their own sakes, they verily eat in sin." The sacrifice called for is mental; one must give up the idea of a personal will, but the results of one's labors need not be sacrificed.

How, asked the ancient writers of the Hindu scriptures, can one have personal knowledge of any value when he knows not the source from whence he came? It is better to become an instrument of the Lord, for then all of man's actions will be right actions and will surely lead to enlightenment.

"Know thou that from Brahma actions groweth ... and the self, deluded by egotism, thinketh, 'I am the doer.' Surrender all actions to Me; with thy thoughts resting on the supreme Self, from hope and egotism freed, from mental fever cured, engage in battle.

"Having abandoned attachment to the fruits of action, always content, his mind and self-controlled, he doth not commit sin. Content with whatever he obtaineth, free from the pairs of opposites, without envy, balanced in success and failure, though acting he is not bound. Even if thou art the most sinful of sinners yet wilt thou cross over all sin by the raft of wisdom.

"On Me fix thy mind; devoted to Me, sacrifice all actions to Me. Harmonized thus in the Self thou shalt come to Me, having Me as thy supreme goal."

This is the great rule of prayerful-action upon which human emancipation depends. Without such Soul communion we become animated robots, producing a mechanical civilization which will destroy itself. Without action a race becomes lost in psychism, and is destroyed by its physical stagnation. There can be no progress when either one or the other is lacking, and this holds for both individuals and nations.

It requires faith and a great deal of courage to abandon the logic on which we have learned to depend. It takes a deep and sincere desire for unity to pray, "Thy will be done, Infinite One." But it is only by such surrender that we can hope to rise above our present limitations. Such sacrifice, said Whitman, is true love and all else is "sounded and resounded words, chattering words, echoes, dead words, the murmurs of incredible dreams."

This kind of sacrifice must be complete and final if it is to be more than a religious gesture, or an effort to escape a particular difficulty. The personal will must be surrendered a hundred times a day; it must become a habit, a new attitude of mind. To breathe the prayer, "Thy will, not mine, be done" means that we are willing to accept the guidance of the cosmic wisdom, welcoming whatever experiences are necessary, knowing there is a divine purpose in every one. It means that we accept the Soul for what it is—the Cause, the Originator, the 'doer'.

True enough we must abandon the childish idea of a personal will, but this also means that we find a new freedom, for if we put our trust in the Soul most decisions will be made for us by the course of events. Events will shape themselves for us, the right doors will open as though by magic and the wrong doors will remain closed. Living more spontaneously we will learn to respond to divine impulse, to inspiration, to intuitive urges, and our actions will always be right. We will learn not to make decisions in advance of need, fretting and scheming in a vain attempt to solve tomorrow's problems today.

It is truly a life of faith and adventure, for we must proceed on faith alone until we become more sensitive to our intuitive faculties. The intricate paths we must follow and the final results of our actions will not be revealed in advance. These are the things the reasoning mind strives for, and they are the warp and woof of most of our worries. The true adventurer does not ask to know such things in advance; this is the chief difference between the reasonable man and the adventurous man. The pathway of adventure, whether it be the exploration of unknown jungle or the limitless ocean of consciousness, must always be a path of faith.

The vast treasures of the new world of consciousness are not for the weak but for the strong—for those capable of casting aside the comfortable traditions and thought patterns of the masses. Here is the greatest challenge which has ever faced any individual and the prize is commensurate with the risk and sacrifices. It is the challenge of life itself, beckoning us on to a freer, more spontaneous existence; urging us to leave the monotonous levels of rationalism for a life of faith and adventure.

But how, we ask, can we know what to do unless we plan and reason and make decisions? We know what to do just as we have always known—by the need of the moment. Every human being, and every animal for that matter, is guided by the realization of need. These various needs are determined by the Soul, but as I have pointed out all "needs" can be divided into two general categories: Those which lead to diversification, the achievement of individuality, and the realization of incompleteness; and those which lead to convergence, unity, and the realization of wholeness.

All of one's experiences are determined by "needs;" they are the guiding factors, the "lines of force" by which the Soul directs destiny. When we begin the return journey—the movement toward a field of consciousness which discloses the inseparable unity of self and Soul—our material needs are not essentially different from what they were before. But there is a greater, overall need which now determines the manner in which our lesser needs shall be supplied. Whereas we have depended on reason, personal will, self-reliance, we must now learn to depend on the wisdom, purpose and power of the Soul.

Nowhere that I know of is the new relationship expressed more effectively than in the verses quoted from the Bhagavad-Gita. Recognizing one's needs one must also recognize the source of all needs and all actions—not occasionally but all the time. In "surrendering actions" we are placing the responsibility where it rightfully belongs, for there are not two powers; there is but one and it is the cosmic Soul. Every belief in personal power is a delusion, the product of an immature form of consciousness which conceives opposing forces. Thus the acceptance of the Soul as the doer is more than a religious gesture; it is the most vital factor governing our emancipation from the world of intellectual darkness. It is a condition imposed on us by the very nature of Being.

The bonds of rational consciousness are so strong that many efforts are required to break them. Habit will reassert itself time and again and we will find ourselves scheming, worrying, trying to forecast the results of our actions, making decisions in advance of need, etc. A more or less continual reorientation is necessary until the old thought-patterns are completely destroyed. Prayer is the most effective instrument through which the surrender of personal autonomy can be made. It is in fact the only instrument, though our concepts of "prayer" may differ. As I employ the term here it means communion with the Soul; it may be either emotional or mental or both, but its purpose is always the same—union with the Soul, a greater realization of the mystery of being. I say either mental or emotional for the unexpressed longings of the heart, the deep and incoherent desires to know reality, are prayers in the truest sense of the word.

Meditation, contemplation, prayer—each has its place and fills a specific need. Through meditation we may employ the principles of dialectic; through detached contemplation we become sensitive to our higher faculties; prayer keeps us attuned to the mystery we do not know, but which we *must* know since it is cause. And it is this latter instrument which becomes our guide to action. To paraphrase the familiar prayer, "Thy will be done on earth as it is in heaven" we might say: "I recognize You, Infinite Soul, as the one power; I know You are the Source of all needs, all actions, and that You have always been, even during the days when I believed I was the doer. Now give me the realization in the midst of activity that you are the doer. Let all of my experiences lead me out of the world of opposites to a realization of oneness."

There will be many slips. Time and again we will find ourselves immersed in the fog of racial beliefs, thinking that we are "something in ourselves"—that we have separate existence and free will. Just as often we must return to the source, for once we have seen the light we will never again be satisfied with the husks of rational existence. Sometimes it will seem that freedom is an illusion and that Reality is a myth, and the rational faculties will convince us that the three-dimensional world is the reality. But it cannot be for long. The deepest desire of the Soul is for reunion, and sooner or later we must again heed the call.

Of the four instruments which enable us to make the transition—meditation, contemplation, prayer, action—none is so potent as prayer. It is always available, day and night, in the midst of activity or in the quiet moments, when we are troubled or at peace. The more intimate and spontaneous it becomes, the more effective it will be, but no matter how we pray we must "pray without ceasing."

Action will never be impersonal but our manner of living can become more spontaneous, and as it does new wonders will appear on every hand, new mysteries will intrigue us, new beauties and harmonies will become manifest. There will be new revelations of cosmic wisdom, new perspectives, intuitive promptings which reveal the straightness of the path. They will come unannounced; hours in the solitude may reveal nothing, yet the coming light is only delayed; when least expected the simplest phenomenon will disclose a mystic secret. Such is the way of the Soul, always mysterious, spontaneous, beyond reason; a way so superior that it must be experienced to be understood, and when understood can never be fully explained.

28

LOVE — THE UNIFYING COSMIC FORCE

IN THE HEBREW SCRIPTURES it is written, "Perfect love casteth out all fear," and again, "Love is the fulfillment of the law." The only kind of love which is capable of overcoming all human fears is that which lifts us to a realm where fear is unknown, and it is the same love which fulfills the law of Being.

This love is an affinity for the Soul, a desire to be embraced and absorbed by the eternal Reality. It is not a tender emotion but a passion which grows from day to day until we long for unity with the Soul as fiercely as any primitive being longs for a mate. It is a love which makes us not only willing to surrender personal autonomy, but makes us willing to accept extinction for even a glimpse of Reality. That which we desire is unknown, but we follow blindly, hopefully, devoutly; accepting the tasks of life without bargaining, and accepting the remuneration without question.

It is not a life devoid of desire, nor the satisfactions which come from work well done, but we no longer delude ourselves as to the relative worth of objective things. The objective life becomes a means to an end and every experience has a two-fold value, the most important of which is a greater realization of unity.

This love is also a demanding passion—always demanding more light, more faith, greater sensitiveness to the promptings of the Soul. It demands Reality itself and will not be satisfied with the crumbs of illumination which come from time to time; it demands reunion, absorption, full knowledge of the great mystery of Being.

This kind of love smolders in the heart of every man and woman who has tried the husks of rational existence and found them empty. Perhaps it is not recognized since it is not the love of the human personality; it is hidden in the Soul and is in reality the power of the cosmos drawing us up to a realization of Being. It is the transcendent love of the cosmic Soul, terrifying in its infiniteness, elevating, omniscient, radiant. It is the love of the Infinite Mother of Gautama, the Father of Jesus, the Lord of David, the Christ of Saint Paul, the Great Laughter of Carpenter, the Friend and Companion of Whitman—the love of a Being who is centered in the hearts of all men and women, and in whom all are immersed.

Concerning love as a cosmic force little can be said that would be acceptable to the intellect. To say that it is the one and only power in the universe means little, for we cannot think except in terms of opposing forces. It appears that love and hate are opposites and that they cannot be manifestations of the same cosmic force. Yet they are, just as the two ends of a stick are one and we cannot determine where the one ends and the other begins.

The patriot comes to the defense of his country because of love, but in the heat of combat that love changes to hate. Every man who seeks financial security is inspired by love for his family and hatred for the condition he is trying to overcome, and one emotion is just as effective as the other. Love, let us say, is the great unifying power of the universe, and it uses two apparently different avenues to achieve the same end, which is union with a new and better condition.

This is certainly true in regard to the achievement of a higher form of consciousness. On the one hand we must destroy our illusions with a ruthless disregard of consequences, and at the same time we must nourish the desire for truth. We must "love God and hate mammon" for while the two emotions seem to be opposites the unknown motive force is the same, and its end or purpose is a greater realization of unity.

We love right action and hate wrong action, and between the two we conceive a great moral difference. Cosmically there is no such thing as moral difference. That which we violate by "wrong action" is the realization of our essential unity, which in itself is neither good nor bad, but inherent and natural. All that any action can do is increase or decrease our realization of this fundamental unity; and as it is our nature to move toward a more complete realization of Being, anything we do that hurts a fellowman hurts us. To state it conversely, anything we do which helps a fellowman increases our realization of this basic unity and therefore helps us. This is the cosmic principle upon which the great ethical codes of the avatars are founded.

Love for our fellowman is therefore a natural requisite for emancipation, but as Jesus pointed out it is the "second law," the first being an overwhelming passion for truth, or the Soul.

It is quite certain that only the adventurous men and women will achieve Cosmic Consciousness, for only the men and women of courage and faith are capable of giving up the old gods and the old idols. Lacking this spirit we must remain in the realm of the known, living by rote and reason. However, the adventurous attitude alone cannot bring illumination. Faith indeed lifts us above the dark levels of rationalism, but faith in the goodness of life is not sufficient; it must be coupled with a great love for the mystic and wondrous—with a growing desire to know the unknown guide.

The quest must never stop short of reality. It is this which so few of us realize. Many of us have the necessary courage and faith for the great adventure, but convinced that we "know God"—that our concepts and ideals of deity are true—our progress is arrested. Until we realize that we do not know, we cannot begin to know. That which we do not know, we cannot begin to know. That which we call God will always be the great mystery. It is still the great mystery to the initiate, to the man or woman who has achieved reunion, who has been absorbed by the Soul, felt its rhythms, beheld its radiance, tasted the nectar of its love, heard the soundless laughter and bathed in its infinite wisdom. Only the ignorant who do not know they are ignorant think they know God, his attributes and characteristics.

Here is the great paradox of Being: The Soul can only be known when we approach it as the unknown, and the more fully we know it the greater its mystery. Thus we are always progressing when we know that we do not know, and spiritual discernment ends the moment we think we know. When emancipation is achieved we find that the Soul is utterly different from all that has ever been written or said about it, from all that we have imagined; and then it is that *knowing* we find ourselves immersed in eternal mystery.

We live in an unknown universe. Of its three-dimensional aspects we know a little which in itself is illusory: of its real nature we know nothing. The little section we now occupy is but one of "many mansions" in a multi-dimensional space, which space is identical with consciousness.

Progress must therefore always be in a new direction, toward a section of space which is circumscribed by a new dimension. This progress involves the acquisition of higher senses, rather than new uses for old faculties.

That reason is the highest power of the third-dimension there can be no question. But that it is not the highest human faculty is also beyond question, for among the more spiritually advanced the intuitive faculties have already made their appearance. And it is these higher faculties which will lead us out of the darkness whenever we make an effort to discredit the reliability and discontinue the use of the old.

The way may be long or short, depending on our willingness to break away from the old. Some will make the transition quickly, for having caught a vision of truth they will pursue it regardless of costs or consequences. As of old it is now, "That the Kingdom of Heaven suffereth violence, and the violent take it by storm." Others by the requirements of their natures will move more cautiously. But for all who set out in this new direction there can be but one guide, and that is the Soul.

It will not be a way of indolence and inaction, nor is it a way of peace, but every step brings us more freedom. And it is the way of miracles; small miracles, perhaps, but miracles nonetheless. Help will come from the most unexpected places and often in unusual ways.

Things will happen to our advantage which are never disadvantageous to another. Events will shape themselves so that decisions are made without effort. Old, unwanted conditions will begin to dissolve, and some will pass away without warning. Relationships with others will be more amicable and old enmities will begin to disintegrate. Knowing that no man or woman can obstruct our path, that the source of all experiences is within, the hold of the competitive principle is broken. We accept the rightful fruits of our actions, realizing that our supply comes forth in answer to our needs, and that the needs themselves originate in the Soul.

We begin to see that all changes exist as realities in a higher section of our Being, that the existing realities in that section are infinite, and that we experience these realities according to our capacity for realizing them.

There is a growing realization of a fluid universe, governed by an infinitely wise and immanent power. More and more the world appears as a mystic unknown which barely conceals its secrets, and someday when we least expect it the veil will be rent and we will be face to face with the living Reality.

Then we will know the meaning of an ecstasy so intense that it often borders on pain, a radiance so brilliant that there are no shadows. Soaring on wings of freedom we shall go where we will, moving more swiftly than light through an unobstructed universe. We will know at last the meaning of laughter and rhythm, and how they are the foundation of the universe. And we shall know the fullness of an indescribable peace, for all sense of becoming is replaced by the realization of Being which is perfect, complete, dynamic.

With the first mystical awakening will come a realization of the cosmos which forever alienates us from the misconceptions of the imagination. Living in the world we will have overcome the world. All questions of the intellect regarding the nature of self, God, the purpose of existence, the meaning of birth and death, will have been answered. We will know that life is eternal, that we are absolutely secure, that our destinies are already written and that they are far more wonderful than we could have conceived.

Returning to the world of three-dimensions the parade of passing events will never again disturb our inner serenity, for in the midst of turmoil we will be able to withdraw to the recesses of Being where persists the realization of timeless, fathomless harmony. Whatever we wish to do will be accomplished easily, for we will do only those things which are compatible with the Self. We will get what we need and with little effort. Compelled by the nature of existence to discriminate, to make decisions, we do so with the realization that there are not two persons or two paths, and that the wisdom of the Soul enters into all of our affairs, guiding us unerringly into peace, usefulness and plenty.

Continuing to be active in the affairs of mankind we are free from the strife and uncertainty which characterizes rational consciousness. Bigness does not impress us for we have witnessed the vastness of Being. The accumulation of wealth does not entice us for we realize our oneness with all. Desire for authority in the world does not afflict us for we know there is but one author and that all men and women are its instruments. Opinions will never again confuse us for we carry with us the knowledge of Reality. And though our knowledge is secret it becomes an ever more vital force that we use in healing, blessing, and inspiring others, reaching them through the mystic avenues of an old-embracing Soul.

The intellect, like instinct and emotion, becomes a more fitting instrument for our higher faculties—an instrument which is ever attuned to the Soul, sensitive to its superior wisdom and the great mystery of Being. Thus we are prepared for further adventures in the world of the wondrous, a realm of Being, wherein aeons of experience will not exhaust its mystery, for it is infinite.

92564574R00118